T0339511

The Power of Leadership Insight

Leadership is a risky business. In the current world, change is the new normal and only constant. As change grows, so does risk. Thus, leaders must be master change agents and master mitigators of risk. But, how will leaders succeed if they don't measure and lack insight? Simply put, they won't. Those that are successful in these arenas will ride the waves of success during their tenure on the leadership stage.

In contrast, their counterparts will be crushed by the never-ending waves of disruption. Often leaders or those aspiring erroneously view leadership power from a self-interested perspective. They see power through the lens of a title, position, control over others, influence, emotional intelligence and the like. Unfortunately, this view is misaligned and short sighted. Another perspective of leadership is the ability to impact positive change for those around you. In reality, leaders are those that use their gifts, skills and knowledge to educate and empower others in the long run.

The purpose of this book is to unveil insight as to the true meaning of leadership power – how to attain it, how to leverage it to add the greatest amount of value to humanity, how to weaponize it to marginalize and eliminate risk and how to share it with others so they can carry the torch once you step off the leadership stage.

In this book, readers will learn:

- How to master the art of change
- The value of leadership self-advocacy
- The pearls and pitfalls of leading integration teams
- The unintended consequences of sharing knowledge
- The sidewinder effect of misinterpreting root causes of success
- The leadership test of humility
- Leadership matchmaking to ensure the right leaders are selected to solve the organization's problems
- Leadership Loopholes: The Houdini Effect
- The risk of underestimating leadership value
- The risk of not focusing on the right attributes
- The risk of leading turnarounds

The Power of Leadership Insight

11 Keys Leaders Must Master to Access Power, Knowledge, and Sustainable Success in High-Risk Environments

Casey J. Bedgood

Routledge
Taylor & Francis Group

A PRODUCTIVITY PRESS BOOK

First published 2024
by Routledge
605 Third Avenue, New York, NY 10158

and by Routledge
4 Park Square, Milton Park, Abingdon, Oxon, OX14 4RN

Routledge is an imprint of the Taylor & Francis Group, an informa business

ISBN: 978-1-032-57382-3 (hbk)
ISBN: 978-1-032-57381-6 (pbk)
ISBN: 978-1-003-43912-7 (ebk)

DOI: 10.4324/9781003439127

Typeset in Garamond
by Deanta Global Publishing Services, Chennai, India

Contents

Author

 **Casey J. Bedgood** is an author, thought leader and master change agent with over 20 years of healthcare leadership experience. He is the author of *The Ride of a Lifetime, The Ideal Performance Improvement Eco System, The ABCs of Designing Performance Improvement Programs, Conquering the Giants, The Power of Organizational Knowledge, Fit for the Fight* and *The Mystery of Leadership.* He is a Six Sigma Black Belt and an accomplished author. Over the years, Casey's work has been recognized, sourced and modeled by National and Global best practice organizations in the healthcare industry and beyond. He has amassed a portfolio of dozens of publications on topics such as: thought leadership, knowledge transfer, performance improvement, strategic design, innovative thinking, transformation, Quality Management System (QMS) and many others. Subsequently, many large complex healthcare enterprises across the US, Canada, the United Kingdom and Singapore have sourced and sought after Casey's thought leadership expertise.

Casey earned a BBA Magna Cum Laude from Mercer University and a Master's in Public Administration from Georgia College & State University (GCSU). He is an Institute of Industrial and Systems Engineers (IISE) Lean Green Belt, Six Sigma Green Belt and Six Sigma Black Belt. Also, Change Acceleration Process (CAP) trained via GE, he is a member of the American College of Healthcare Executives (ACHE) and member of the Institute of Industrial and Systems Engineers (IISE).

Introduction

If you only had a year left in your career as a leader, what would you spend your time doing? Would you spend more time in meetings? Would you invest more time on conference calls and in conversations arguing points that won't be relevant beyond the year's end? Would you spend time playing politics for the next level role or competing with peers to get ahead?

The genesis of this book is over two decades of experience working with leaders from all over the world in various industries. The one common denominator is that all leaders are human. Moreover, we are all constrained by time. Simply put, time is finite. Once a day is gone we don't get it back and we are never guaranteed another day. Our careers and tenure in leadership roles are not indefinite. The career journey has two guarantees: a starting point and an end. No one has a forever clock.

Thus, leaders must spend their time wisely focusing on leading instead of all the needless and non-value adding activity that engrosses the life of most leaders. It's remarkable how many years leaders spend on the hamster wheel politicking, in vying for next level roles, in meetings, on justifying decisions and the like. Is this really the best use of a leader's time? Arguably not.

If your career ended by the year's end, what would you leave behind for the next generation of leaders to follow? What would others say about your contribution to the industry, to the body of knowledge, to their lives and to the generations to come? Would they even remember you six months from now?

Recently, a CEO of a large service organization retired abruptly after a multi-decade career in various leadership positions. This leader was a national leader in many ways. They spent countless hours on the career hamster wheel, in meetings, in traveling, on giving speeches, in mastering the art of politics and on attempting to influence others to support their point of view.

After retiring, the leader exited the career stage and essentially disappeared over night. Within six months most staff and former direct reports barely remembered who the leader was. All the accolades and influence were gone and self-reflection for those that witnessed the scenario was in order. In short, was this multi-decade career the best use of time? Although there were many notable accomplishments, it's safe to say it was not entirely the best path.

The purpose of this book is to unveil insight as to the true meaning of leadership power – how to attain it, how to leverage it to add the greatest amount of value to humanity, how to weaponize it to marginalize and eliminate risk and, finally, how to share it with others so they can carry the torch once you step off the leadership stage.

Often leaders or those aspiring erroneously view leadership power from a self-interested perspective. They see power through the lens of a title, position, control over others, influence, emotional intelligence and the like. Unfortunately, this view is misaligned and short sighted.

In its simplest form, leadership is getting others to do what you want without force. Another perspective of leadership is the ability to impact positive change for those around you. In reality, leaders are those that use their gifts, skills and knowledge to empower others in the long run.

The ultimate test of a leader depends on:

- How many people will follow you?
- How many will remember you once you have exited the leadership stage?
- How many people did you help during your leadership tenure?
- How much knowledge did you share and leave behind for the next generation?

In *The Power of Leadership Insight*, readers will learn how to master the art of change, the value of leadership self-advocacy, the pearls and pitfalls of leading integration teams, the unintended consequences of sharing knowledge, the side winder effect of misinterpreting root causes of success, the leadership test of humility, leadership match making to ensure the right leaders are selected to solve the organization's problems, the risk of underestimating leadership value, the risk of not focusing on the right attributes and the risk of leading turnarounds.

Leadership is a risky business. In today's world, change is the new normal and only constant. As change grows, so does risk. Thus, leaders must be master change agents and master mitigators of risk. But, how will leaders succeed if they don't measure and lack insight? Simply put, they won't.

Those that are successful in these arenas will ride the waves of success during their tenure on the stage. In contrast, their counterparts will be crushed by the never-ending waves of disruption.

This book is one of several contributions to the leadership body of knowledge. It is being written for students, leaders, those aspiring thought leaders and change agents, and anyone interested in the art of leadership. The reality is that leadership is both an art and a science. If either is lacking from the leadership portfolio, success will only be a pipe dream instead of a viable reality.

Therefore, insight has great power. Arguably the wisest person to ever live, King Solomon wrote, 'A wise man has great power' (Proverbs 24:5) and 'Wisdom makes one wise man more powerful than ten rulers in a city' (Ecclesiastes 7:19). This book will help unlock the code to the power of leadership insight and enlighten the right path for success.

1

Mastering the Art of Change: Is the Hassle Worth the Risk?

CHANGE ATTRIBUTES

In today's world, change is the new normal and only constant. As change grows, so does the associated risk. By definition, change occurs when something is made different (*Merriam-Webster*). There is an art and science to change. The science persona of change relates to data, measuring, testing statistical significance and other attributes that help leaders verify that the current state is different.

In contrast, the art of change involves intellectual decision making on many fronts. The art persona of change is where thought leaders and change agents use discernment, skill and insight to make decisions. These decisions can relate to potential solutions for problems, aligning culture to change initiatives so the change sticks long term, managing relationships and determining which initiatives are high or low risk. Risk applies to the organization, its stakeholders and the change agent.

There are several attributes of change worth noting for this discussion. The first attribute relates to change types. Incremental change occurs over time. This change type is typically very slow and allows stakeholders to adapt to the change slowly. Thus, it's often more palatable and easier to adjust to in many instances.

There is also transformational change. This change type is fast and disruptive. Here, stakeholders have very little time to adjust to the new operating environment. Also, the transformational nature of this change type creates a radically different new normal. Thus, it's very disruptive and very high risk.

DOI: 10.4324/9781003439127-1

Scope is also another change attribute. For this conversation, scope applies to the organization or its subparts. Some change impacts the entire enterprise. Other changes may only impact a division or collection of departments under the same operating umbrella. The least impactful scope of change only impacts a single department.

The key to change is time. Will the change last or dissolve quickly? Some change initiatives realize wins that are sustained long term (typically several years or more). Other change activities only realize wins that are successful short term (typically lasting less than a year). Unfortunately, some change never realizes wins or attains predetermined goals.

With any change, there is always a reaction. One of the most important questions change agents should ask is, how will stakeholders react to change? There are several reactions for which change agents should be prepared when implementing change, particularly in high-risk environments. The reaction spectrum ranges from stakeholders championing the change to being in complete denial that change is needed. (See Figure 1.1 for details.)

Some stakeholders will champion change and function as a positive sounding board. Here, the leaders voluntarily model or lead the change to ensure its success. Also, they play a crucial role in aligning the culture to the change initiative. This is imperative for any wins to stick long term.

Some stakeholders simply accept the change. Here, the leaders and other stakeholders are glad or joyful. They are excited about the change with hopes

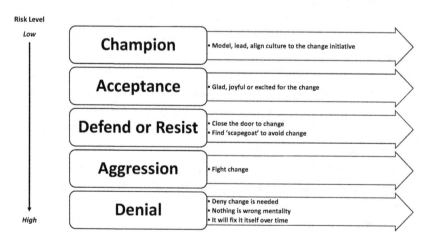

FIGURE 1.1

Change reaction spectrum.

that the change will create a better operating landscape. Both champions and acceptors of change are relatively lower risk to change success.

The third level on the change spectrum relates to defenders or resisters. Here, the stakeholders attempt to close the door to change. The number one reaction is to find a scapegoat to cover the true root cause of the need for change. Think of a pull culture where leaders know they have issues, but push improvement resources away instead of embracing help to change and solve issues.

The fourth level of change reaction is aggression. Here stakeholders including leaders fight or resist the change at every cost. This is a very risky and dangerous change landscape. Change agents must immediately mitigate the aggressor and ensure change sabotage does not occur.

Finally, some stakeholders exhibit denial when faced with change. The mentality is, 'Nothing is wrong' or 'The issue will resolve itself over time.' This too is a very risky operating landscape as stakeholders deny change is needed.

This information is great. But, there is one glaring omission. What about the change agent perspective? Looking back on years of change agent training and implementations, we were never taught risks for the change agents themselves. In most Lean or Six Sigma courses, for example, the foci are to train, pass the exam, succeed in improvement projects, amass a list of cross functional wins, resume build and save a lot of money. Unfortunately, very little if any time is spent preparing change agents for the 'art' of change.

The 'art' is very important to the long-term success of the organization and the change agent as an individual. Specifically, there are four risks change agents should consider for themselves when agreeing to pursue, accept, lead or participate in change initiatives. The first question change agents should ask themselves is, 'Is the initiative a relationship builder?' Will the initiative add value to the change agent's brand and relationships and provide solutions for others?

The second risk consideration is, 'Will my participation in this event be a relationship ender?' Here, the change initiative may expose sensitive operational information for leaders they wish to keep from the public view. Inadvertently, the change agent will be required to identify and magnify these issues during the process. The real question is if the risk is worth the reward. Simply put, can you live without the relationship if it ends due to the engagement?

The third consideration relates to the change agent's career. Is the event a career ender? It's one thing to lose a relationship over a change initiative.

But, it's a whole different equation when one's career is jeopardized. Here, the biggest risk is losing political capital or tarnishing one's brand as a result of the engagement. Although the outcomes may be positive in the short run, the consideration here is on the long-term consequences.

The fourth risk consideration is, 'Will my participation in the engagement be a career builder?' Career builders help change agents amass wins, build credibility, enhance the brand and gain skill plus respect in the role. There are both upside and downside risks with career builder engagements. The upside is the positive career gains previously mentioned. The downside is tied directly to the relationship side of the equation.

Let's take a practical look at a real-world example.

CASE IN POINT

A large service organization began training top leaders in change methodologies such as Lean, Six Sigma and others. With time, the training penetrated lower leadership levels and even reached the front lines. The initial intent was to train change agents, deploy them throughout the enterprise to address waste and realize hard dollar savings. Unfortunately, most leaders and front-line staff never adopted the methodology post training.

For most, the change agent credential was just another plaque on the wall. But, there were a few change agents that mastered the art and science of change engagements. They quickly amassed significant cross functional wins, saved large sums of hard dollars and were recognized as national leaders in the craft. As time passed, one senior leader gravitated to one of the high-flying change agents.

Every time the organization experienced an impossible operational issue, the senior leader pulled out the sling shot (theoretically speaking), loaded the change agent and shot them into the chaos. Time and time again the change agent was successful in leading long-term improvements that no one else could achieve. There was no issue that the change agent would not engage regardless of scope, size or risk. These outcomes gained national recognition in various respected industry venues. But, no one including the change agent considered the collateral damage along the journey.

The focus was solely on solving problems, positively impacting humanity, saving dollars and creating solutions that stood the test of time. Everyone should celebrate and be excited about this success. Right? Unfortunately, that is not always the case.

As time passed, leadership changes occurred. The change agent found themselves maneuvering in a new operating landscape with new leadership. The change agent's reputation preceded them. But, not everyone celebrated all the success.

In retrospect, the change agent used a simple risk assessment tool to determine why the success attracted some and repelled others. The findings are in Figure 1.2.

For the look back, the change agent assessed five large change engagements for their risk and ideal action plans in retrospect. The risk assessment tool has five attributes:

1. What's the change engagement's relationship potential? Is it a relationship builder or relationship ender?
2. Is the engagement a potential career builder or career ender?
3. What impact will the change have on humanity related to life, health or safety?
4. What is the return on investment (ROI) related to value for each change? Value focuses on improvements or lack thereof in service levels, cost and quality of services.
5. What's the scope of the change? Scope focuses on whether the change will impact the organization as a whole, a division or just a department.

In short, those initiatives that are career or relationship enders are higher risk. In contrast, career and relationship building changes are lower risk. The changes that produce greater value for the organization, its people and the customers are lower risk. Those changes that impact more of the organization are higher risk.

As noted in Figure 1.2, initiatives 1, 2, and 3 were the most successful. All three were career and relationship builders as they added great value to all stakeholders. These engagements help build positive relationships with other leaders and teams. Also, they produced the greatest positive impact on humanity and the highest operational return on investment. It's important to note that all three impacted the entire enterprise. Globally, they were all low-risk change engagements. Thus, the change agent was justified in 'taming the bull' by aggressively pursuing and leading these initiatives.

Initiative	Relationship Potential 1-Relationship Builder 2-Relationship Ender	Career Potential 1-Career Builder 2-Career Ender	Impact on Humanity (Life, Health, Safety) 1- Positive Impact 2- No Impact 3- Negative Impact	Return on Investment (Service, Quality, Cost) 1- Adds Value 2- No Value Add	Change Scope 1-Department 2-Division 3-Organization Wide	Risk Score *Sum Columns 2-6 Lower Score = Lower Risk	Action Plan
Initiative 1	1	1	1	1	3	7	Tame the Bull
Initiative 2	1	1	1	1	3	7	Tame the Bull
Initiative 3	1	1	1	1	3	7	Tame the Bull
Initiative 4	2	2	2	2	1	9	Proceed with Caution
Initiative 5	2	2	3	2	3	12	Run for the Hills
Avg Score	1.4	1.4	1.6	1.4	2.6		
Risk Level	Low Risk	Low Risk	Low Risk	Low Risk	High Risk		

Lowest Risk 5
Max Risk 12
Avg Risk 9

FIGURE 1.2

Risk assessment tool.

Initiative 4 had a slightly different risk proposition. Here, the engagement had good potential to be a relationship and career ender due to sensitive operational details that had to be exposed during the change process. It also had no impact on humanity and had no value return related to improvements in service, cost or quality. Surprisingly, the scope was least risky as only a department was involved. Overall, the initiative was average risk. Thus, the change agent should have proceeded with caution instead of running into the fire full steam ahead.

Finally, initiative 5 was the highest risk overall. Here, the engagement had the potential to be a career and relationship ender if things went awry. Also, the change's impact on humanity was negative and the initiative provided no value related to service, cost or quality. Moreover, the change scope impacted the entire organization. Overall, the change agent should have run for the hills and avoided this opportunity as the risk exceeded the potential reward.

Looking back, only 60% of the initiatives were low risk and a good choice.

SUMMARY

So, what was learned from the case study and risk assessment? One, change is a risky proposition and there is a cost for every engagement. Two, what sparkles does not always shine. Change agents must understand the risk and reward for leading, participating in and pursuing improvement opportunities. Three, ignorance is never bliss. Leaders and change agents don't know what they don't measure. Unfortunately, unmitigated risks will eventually unfavorably impact leaders, organizations and their customers. Thus, a simple risk assessment tool is warranted.

Finally, the million-dollar question all change agents must answer for themselves is, 'Is it worth being a fixer?' Simply put, is the reward for being an unbridled change agent greater than the risk? The answer is both simple and complex. On the positive side, the answer is yes if the engagement improves humanity, adds value, grows relationships and increases organizational knowledge. The answer is no if the change initiative collectively is a sure career and relationship ender, adds no value and negatively impacts humanity.

The reality is simple. Even in the best of circumstances, change agents will garner friends and foes. At the end of the day, effective leaders of change must focus on what is most important. A focus on risk, humanity, value and increasing knowledge far outweighs any detractors realized or lost as a result of change initiatives.

The art of mastering change is measuring frequently, mitigating risk, leveraging relationships, cutting the dead weight detractors and ensuring value is added at every corner. Effective leaders are those master change agents that ensure the reward of change exceeds the risks each and every time.

2

The Value of Leadership Self-Advocacy

SPHERES OF ADVOCACY

Per Merriam-Webster, advocacy is the 'act or process of supporting a cause or proposal' (1). Often, leaders are involved in the advocacy process for themselves and others. Typically, these leaders are often tagged with the term 'sponsor.' A sponsor is 'a person who takes the responsibility for some other person or thing' (1). In layman's terms, a leadership sponsor is one who uses their experience, influence and skillset to leverage situations for the benefit of others.

Sponsors typically operate in two spheres. (See Figure 2.1 for details.)

The first sphere of advocacy relates to internal advocacy. Internal advocacy pertains to sponsorship inside the organization. Here, leaders tend to advocate for people or agendas in three categories.

The first category is vertical. This attribute relates to the organizational chart. Leaders may advocate with superiors or subordinates, for example. In this scenario, a leader may advocate for support from superiors to increase funding for a project. Another example could be advocacy for approval of capital funds to buy a new piece of machinery that costs several million dollars. From a people perspective, often leaders that are good sponsors advocate for their subordinates when promotions or learning opportunities present themselves. This may come in the form of the leader placing a good word for their subordinate to other hiring leaders higher on the organizational chart.

The second category of internal advocacy relates to a horizontal perspective. Here, leaders may advocate with or for peers. Often, organizations use 360 reviews during promotions, for example. In this scenario, other leaders from areas outside the leadership candidate's business unit are interviewed for insight as to whether the candidate is ready for the next level, can work

DOI: 10.4324/9781003439127-2

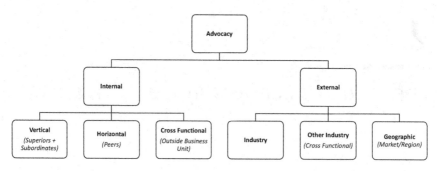

FIGURE 2.1
Spheres of advocacy.

well with others, can produce outcomes and the like. Irrespective of context, horizontal advocacy occurs at the same level of the organizational chart.

The third category of internal advocacy pertains to the cross functional arena. Here, leaders may advocate with leaders in other business units. Topics may include advocacy to have a leader's subordinates placed on teams that are implementing a new change. Another example of this advocacy may involve a leader advocating with peer leaders in other business units for support on projects. There are many examples, but the takeaway is that leaders often find themselves advocating for their people or initiatives with other business units outside of their scope of practice.

The second sphere of advocacy is external advocacy. Hence, the term 'external' implies that the focus is on advocating outside of the organization. There are three subparts to this sphere as well: industry, other industry and geographic. The first subpart is industry advocacy. Here, leaders may advocate for themselves, their organizations or their people in industry respected venues. A simple example is a leader that creates a best practice concept, pilots the concept in their organization, proves the concept to be significant and presents the findings at industry symposiums. The key is that the focus is sponsorship at the industry level and outside the leader's organization.

The second subpart of external advocacy relates to other industries outside the leader's scope of business. A simple example here would be a healthcare leader that is a performance improvement expert. The leader develops an improvement concept that is applicable in manufacturing. After proving the concept is viable via data analysis, the leader publishes it in a book and represents the concept to other leaders in a different industry.

The third subpart of external advocacy relates to a geographic focus. Here, leaders may advocate outside their base organization with stakeholders in another region or market, for example. A simple example would be a multi-state healthcare organization with operations in various markets. Leaders in one market may advocate for their initiatives, people or base hospital with leaders from other markets in the same enterprise. Irrespective of focus, this advocacy takes on a geographic nature.

SPONSORSHIP

In order for advocacy to work, the right people must be present, linked and motivated to advocate for something other than themselves. Thus, sponsors are the grease for the skids that ensure advocacy is successful. When ideal sponsors are present and active, the leadership journey can be much easier. When sponsors are missing or not engaged in the advocacy process, leaders may struggle to find the required helping hand along the career journey that is needed to succeed. Since sponsorship is so important, there are several considerations worth noting.

Are all leaders good sponsors? Is sponsorship as simple as leveraging political capital? Are all sponsors the same? Is it possible for a sponsor to be a waste of time for other respective leaders needing assistance? Can sponsors add only marginal benefit to those around them or is each sponsor a sure bet for success? Is it possible for a sponsor to be a poor fit even though they have higher than average levels of influence? Are there other options for leaders seeking sponsorship if no good fit is available? We will answer these and other considerations in the following.

So how would one know if a leader is a good sponsor? Let's take a look at Figure 2.2 for details.

When assessing a potential or existing sponsor, there are two basic rules of thumb worth noting. One is influence and the other is the leader's interest in advocating for others. As noted in Figure 2.2, leaders that have influence and advocate for others are the ideal sponsor. These sponsors are the best use of one's time for advocacy focus areas. In contrast, those leaders that have influence with others, but lack a drive to advocate are a poor fit. Thus, they should be avoided if possible.

Leaders that don't have influence and don't advocate for others are a waste of time. Here, leaders should look for another viable sponsor versus wasting their time. Finally, those sponsors that advocate for others and possess

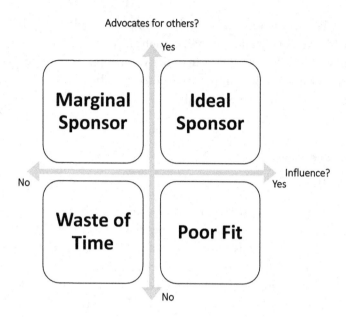

FIGURE 2.2
Sponsor matrix.

little influence are marginal at best. This simply means they may be a good motivator or counselor, but are not the best fit for sponsorship. In layman's terms, the value from partnering with this sponsor is marginal or minimal at best. The relationship would simply be a good conversation that is light on outcomes.

Once leaders have filtered out those sponsors with potential from those that are not a good fit, another level of assessment may be helpful. (See Figure 2.3 for details.)

Here, sponsors are assessed on a variety of attributes. The end goal is for leaders to find and partner with the least risky sponsors as possible. This will ensure the greatest chance of success.

Figure 2.3 is a risk assessment tool for sponsorship. As noted, in this example there are five sponsors. Each is assessed on several attributes: their outcomes, sustained wins, scope of influence, advocacy interest, cross functional wins both inside and outside the organization and published outcomes. Those leaders with lower risk scores are lower risk sponsors. Thus, they pose the greatest probability of success for leaders to partner with them. Those higher risk sponsors should be avoided at all costs.

	Measurable + Significant Outcomes? 1-Yes 2-No	Sustained Wins? 1-Yes 2-No	Scope of Influence 1- Industry 2- Enterprise Wide 3- Divisional 4-Departmental	Advocacy Interest 1-Proactive 2-Neutral 3-No Interest	Internal Cross Functional Wins? 1-Yes 2-No	External Cross Functional Wins? 1-Yes 2-No	Published Outcomes? 1-Yes 2-No	Risk Score *Sum Columns 2-8 Lower Score = Lower Risk	Action Plan
Sponsor 1	1	1	1	1	1	1	1	7	Ideal Sponsor
Sponsor 2	2	2	2	2	2	2	2	14	Waste of Time
Sponsor 3	2	2	3	3	2	2	2	16	Waste of Time
Sponsor 4	1	1	3	2	2	2	2	13	Waste of Time
Sponsor 5	1	2	4	2	1	1	1	12	Proceed with Caution
Avg Score	1.4	1.6	2.6	2.0	1.6	1.6	1.6		
Risk Level	Low Risk	Low Risk	High Risk	High Risk	Low Risk	Low Risk	Low Risk		

FIGURE 2.3

Sponsor risk tool.

Let's take a practical look at the sponsor risk tool. Five leaders are assessed on each attribute. Only one of the leaders is an ideal fit for sponsorship. This leader attained positive operational outcomes that were measurable, statistically significant and sustained long term. This leader also had the highest scope of influence as being recognized as an industry leader. Moreover, they were proactive in advocating for others and amassed respectable operational wins in areas outside their business unit and organization. Finally, they were successful in publishing these outcomes in industry best practice venues. Thus, this sponsor is the ideal fit.

Three of the sponsors were rated as a waste of time. These leaders struggled with outcomes that were measurable, statistically significant and passed the test of time. They also only had influence inside the organization and limited interest at best of advocating for others. None of these leaders were able to publish their work outside the organization to expand the industry body of knowledge. Thus, they are not a good fit for sponsorship.

Finally, the last leader was rated as a marginal sponsor. Here the leader was able to produce significant outcomes in various venues. But, sustaining those wins was an issue. Also, their advocacy interest was neutral, meaning they advocate only if needed. Thus, this sponsor is not a waste of time. They also are not the best choice, either. If no other ideal sponsor was available, then leaders could entertain a partnership with this sponsor with caution, understanding moderate risk levels exist.

The takeaway from the sponsor risk tool is that leaders don't know what they don't measure. Also, what sparkles does not always shine. Often, sponsors appear to be a good fit from the outside looking in due to one attribute. But, when cross comparisons of various attributes are conducted ideal sponsors are quickly filtered out of the pack.

SELF-ADVOCACY

That being said, a lack of sponsorship often forces leaders to self-advocate. Often, leaders advocate for themselves on many fronts. One, leaders may advocate for promotions in some instances. Two, they may advocate for the status quo to preserve current environments that work best in the face of change. Three, leaders may often self-advocate to preserve their roles when organizational restructures occur.

Irrespective of the focus, self-advocacy has risks. There is always a risk that leaders may over advocate for themselves. The pitfall to avoid is over promising and under delivering. It's tempting to play politics and leverage emotional intelligence for one's betterment, but being able to deliver outcomes is the ultimate test of a leader.

Another risk of self-advocacy is producing a mixed message. In today's world, leaders are expected to build teams, grow the pie for others and the like. By self-advocating, leaders must ensure they avoid the pitfall of over emphasizing 'I' or 'me'. Instead, they must showcase their accomplishments or capabilities in concert with the 'us' and 'we' focus. In other words, show how they have succeeded via building teams, synergies and cohesiveness.

The third risk of self-advocacy is twofold. When leaders self-advocate, they run the risk of team degradation or losing trust with peers and subordinates. If others view the leader's self-advocacy as 'they are only out for themselves,' then it's a high-risk situation. Similarly, if leaders don't self-advocate when gaps are present, then they can miss opportunities or lose their current status.

The key is finding balance between objective outcomes, the desire to grow the pie for others and letting performance speak for itself. Let's take a look at a real example.

Case in Point

A large service organization began to experience operational declines for consecutive years. Thus, the revolving door in the top leadership ranks began to spin. The industry average turnover for top leaders during the time was less than 15%. But, the enterprise was experiencing top leadership turnover nearly double the industry average.

As a result, the organization was faced with a merger. A larger corporation folded the enterprise into its operational portfolio. As was expected, over a 2-year period more top leaders began to leave. With the outflow of leaders and the global organizational restructure both occurring at the same time, many leadership gaps and gray areas formed. Think of rats jumping off a sinking ship. It was everyone for themselves essentially.

As these transitions occurred, sponsorship was obsolete and nowhere to be found. Several leaders that were top performers shifted into self-advocacy mode. As the restructure was planned, they unfortunately had no one representing their current roles or rightful position in the newly formed organization. A downside of the leadership gaps also emerged.

Top performing leaders became over competitive with one another trying to vie for the vacant top spots. Team members with long standing working relationships began to compete against each other unhealthily which eroded cohesiveness, trust, synergy and outcomes even further. As some lower performing leaders over advocated for themselves, they essentially over magnified their abilities, skills and performance. They unfortunately leveraged the gaps to achieve promotions and stretch assignments.

The outcomes were not good. Many leaders over promised and under delivered. Their quest to come out on top of their peers and colleagues unraveled high performing teams and shifted the dynamic to the I or me perspective. One leader rose above the storm and used Figure 2.4 to win the battles and wars during the transitions.

As noted in the figure, there were five leaders competing for top spots as the organization was restructured. With regard to self-advocacy, 60% of the group was high risk, 20% low risk and 20% average risk. The top leader that self-advocated properly was Leader 1. This leader has operational outcomes that were measurable, sustained and statistically significant. They also possess an integrated skill set comprising technical and operational leadership and performance improvement credentials with significant outcomes. The key is skills plus 'significant' outcomes validated by data. Leader 1 was also recognized in various industries and cross functional venues of the organization as an industry leader. Moreover, Leader 1 published these outcomes in international best practice venues. The adage of 'the proof is in the pudding' applies here.

The other leaders that over advocated for themselves were not so lucky. As noted in the figure, three of the five leaders should have never self-advocated. They simply did not have the proper combination of skills, outcomes and published wins to validate their self-reflections. The adage of being 'a hero in your own mind' applies here. Thus, they were the highest risk self-advocates and produced the greatest amount of damage to the organization, to themselves and to the teams they led.

Leader 5 was an average risk self-advocate. This leader produced significant outcomes that were sustained long term. But, they lacked an integrated skill set. Moreover, this leader failed to achieve cross functional wins or publish their work. Thus, the leader should have proceeded with caution in self-advocacy to avoid the I or me bias or over promising what they could not deliver if promoted prematurely.

Leader	Measurable Outcomes? 1-Yes 2-No	Sustained Wins? 1-Yes 2-No	Skill Set 1- Technical + Operations + Performance Improvement 2- Technical + Operations 3- Technical	Significant Outcomes? 1-Yes 2-No	Internal Cross Functional Wins? 1-Yes 2-No	External Cross Functional Wins? 1-Yes 2-No	Published Outcomes? 1-Yes 2-No	Risk Score *Sum Columns 2-8 Lower Score = Lower Risk	Action Plan
Leader 1	1	1	1	1	1	1	1	7	Self Advocate
Leader 2	2	2	2	2	2	2	2	14	Don't Advocate
Leader 3	2	2	3	2	2	2	2	15	Don't Advocate
Leader 4	1	1	3	2	2	2	2	13	Don't Advocate
Leader 5	1	1	2	1	2	2	2	11	Proceed with Caution
Avg Score	1.4	1.4	2.2	1.6	1.8	1.8	1.8		
Risk Level	Low Risk	Low Risk	High Risk	Low Risk	Low Risk	Low Risk	Low Risk		

FIGURE 2.4

Self advocacy risk tool.

So, what was learned from the case study? One, advocacy is a risky business. There are both upside and downside risks when self-advocacy occurs. Some leaders self-advocated when they should not have and destroyed teams. In contrast, the low-risk leader self-advocated and won the competition war for the next level role.

Two, leaders don't know what they don't measure. Ignorance is never bliss. Thus, leaders must risk assess their self-advocacy potential before taking the journey. A simple risk tool is an essential template for leaders to use when assessing risk levels for self-promotion. Those in the know will win while those that lack knowledge will step in the pothole.

SUMMARY

Looking back, a simple concept such as advocacy can be complicated. Unfortunately, self-advocacy is not always a choice or as simple as it sounds. Leaders may find themselves in situations where they are their own best and only advocate. If they don't advocate, they will ultimately lose positions, promotions and the like. If they do advocate, it's a high-risk proposition fraught with many potential potholes. But, with big risk comes big reward if leaders respond appropriately.

The takeaway is that all leaders are not good sponsors. Some are a good fit while others are a waste of time. The key is discernment. Effective leaders are those that can assess, measure, mitigate and ultimately avoid high-risk sponsors. When sponsorship is void, leaders must advocate for themselves. The value in self-advocacy is allowing performance, outcomes and objectively measurable capabilities to speak for themselves. Otherwise, non-credible self-advocacy is simply over promising what one can never deliver.

REFERENCE

1. Merriam-Webster, 2022.

3

The Pearls and Pitfalls of Leading Integration Teams

INTEGRATION DEFINED

Is integration work a risky business? Will combining teams, departments or organizations always work flawlessly? Can missteps in combining operations and talent be a career ender? Is culture the only risk factor to consider when bringing teams together or are other pitfalls present? Is a formula for success needed when combining talent and organizations? Can any leader succeed in integrating teams or are some attributes better than others? We will discuss these and many other considerations in the following.

Integration, as it relates to teams, departments and organizations, is synonymous with familiar terms such as 'mergers,' 'combinations' and 'restructures.' Formally, integration can be defined as 'to form, coordinate, or blend into a functioning or unified whole' (1). The whole purpose of integrating teams is to achieve synergy. Synergy is simply accomplishing more together than apart. Technically, synergy is 'the increased effectiveness that results when two or more people or businesses work together' (1).

INTEGRATION PEARLS (BENEFITS)

There are other advantages or intended ends of integrating operational structures. The first advantage is economies of scale. Here, leaders aim to accomplish more with less. Simply put, the organization hopes to reduce operating costs by streamlining the structures. This advantage is often

DOI: 10.4324/9781003439127-3

realized by eliminating or reducing redundant functions, roles, technology and tasks, just to name a few.

Another advantage of integration is value. Value is anything a customer is willing to pay for (2). The value equation relates in simplest terms to quality, service and cost. Regardless of industry, the ultimate measure of success is meeting and exceeding customer requirements. Thus, maximizing the value received by the customer at each touch point or interaction with the company.

A third advantage of combining structures is growth. Here, leaders and governance structures hope to increase the organization's market share or footprint. The end goal is to gain competitive advantages in the market. Growth is typically derived from nimble and synergistic operating structures that add value while minimizing costs. As a result, the organization can outpace competitors and grow its market share.

INTEGRATION RISK FACTORS

Irrespectively, integration has both risks and rewards. These activities can be very risky if not managed appropriately. There are several integration risk factors worth noting. One, integration success or failure is dependent upon the scope of the activity. Does the integration or combination of structures impact the entire enterprise, a division or a single department?

The larger the scope, the greater the risk. (See Figure 3.1 for details.) Enterprise level integration work is most risky as it has the greatest scope which impacts more people and operational arenas. Divisional level and departmental integration activities are associated with less risk as the scope of the work affects fewer people and operational aspects of the organization.

Two, the risk of integration activities depends on the impact potential. There are several considerations worth noting. Will integration impact life and safety? Will the restructure impact the organization's mission? Are the integration impacts only important and not impactful to life, safety or mission? The greater the impact on life, safety and mission, the greater the risk. Thus, leaders must plan accordingly to minimize the risks.

Three, integration work is greatly dependent upon the current state operating environment. Here, leaders must assess the stability of the organization. Is the organization unstable as it relates to the value equation? Are services and quality less than desired by the customer base? Are costs higher than market

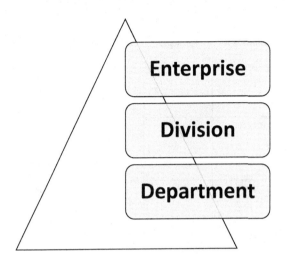

FIGURE 3.1
Integration levels.

competitors or the industry average for the respective operation? The greater the instability, the greater the risk.

The fourth risk factor for integration success relates to sponsorship. Here, leaders and their organizations must assess the top leaders and change agents assigned to integration activities. A sponsor is a leader chosen to lead change, improvements and alignment of structures as needed to achieve market advantages as previously noted. There are several considerations worth noting.

Are the sponsors proactive as it relates to change? Do they proactively engage change, improvement and new ways of doing business or are they neutral to this activity? Are the sponsors disengaged and only sponsor change or improvements if required to do so? The key here is the more engaged sponsorship is, the less risk exists for integration success.

The next risk factor for integration activity is culture. Culture represents the people who do the work in the organization. In layman's terms, culture is how work is done in an enterprise. The key here is for leaders to determine how resistant or accepting the organization is to change. If the culture is change acceptant, then risk is low. If the organization is change neutral or resistant, then the risk is higher.

The final integration risk factor is available talent. Here, leaders must understand the organization's talent canvas. Simple considerations leaders must take account of are as follows. For the areas involved in the integration activity, do strategically oriented staff and leaders exist? Are those affected by

	Function 1	Function 2	Function 3	Function 4	Function 5
Strategic				Thought Leader	
Operational	Director Manager	Director Manager	Director Manager	Director Manager	Director Manager
Tactical	Staff	Staff	Staff	Staff	Staff

- Strategic: Integrated skill set (Technical/Ops/PI w/ significant cross functional outcomes)
- Operational: Day to day dept. level leadership
- Tactical: Boots on the ground/front line work

FIGURE 3.2
Integration matrix (roles/structure).

the integration work operationally minded? Are the talents mainly equipped with tactical knowledge and perspectives? (See Figure 3.2 for details.)

Strategic knowledge relates to one who possesses an integrated skill set. Here, the leader has technical, operational and performance improvement skills with measurable outcomes in cross functional arenas. The adage of thought leaders is well suited for this leadership archetype. These change agents are unique in that they can see the forest for the trees or focus on the big picture while understanding micro-operational elements.

Operational talent tends to focus mainly on the day-to-day departmental level leadership tasks. These functions may include, but may not be limited to, managing small groups of people, limited budgets and making decisions that have a limited impact on the organization's operational canvas. Although important, the impact here is limited. The adage of 'working in the weeds' is applicable here.

Tactical minded talent tends to pertain to the front-line staff and in some cases leadership. These talent pools represent the largest portion of the organization's culture and operating norms. Simply put, tactical talent is required to get work done. Without them, the organization will not run and change will not stick.

The key for integration to work as intended is having a blended matrix comprising strategic, operational and tactical talent as noted in Figure 3.2. Without the proper distribution of talent, the integration work will be high risk. Thus, the probability of failure will be greater. In this instance more is not better and balance is the ideal integration state.

INTEGRATION FORMULA FOR SUCCESS

There is a simple starting point or formula for success in integration work that thought leaders should consider. (See Figure 3.3 for details.)

To succeed in integrating people groups and structures, leaders must first consider people. The first place to start is to consider Maslow's Hierarchy of Needs.

Step one is for leaders to put themselves in the shoes of those impacted by the change. A few considerations are as follows. Will the change impact the ability of staff and leaders to meet basic needs such as food, clothing and shelter for themselves and dependents? Will the change affect one's reputation, position or status in the organization, community or even personally? Will the change allow each person affected to reach their full potential and maximize the use of their talent? If the integration jeopardizes any of the above, then the risks will be higher, resistance to change will be greater and leaders must plan ahead proactively to ensure the change does not become disruptive.

As noted in Figure 3.3, leaders must next consider the operating structure. Here, sponsors and change agents must carefully consider the operating structure. The greater the change to the current operating structure, the greater the risk and likelihood of disruptive outcomes. Again, leaders must plan ahead to ensure the future state structure post integration makes sense, will work and meets the needs of all affected stakeholders. If something is

FIGURE 3.3
Formula for success.

working, why change it? This is the number one consideration change agents must take into account and plan for when designing integration structures. Most common foci here are organizational and functional charts.

The third success formula component is the process. A good process is outlined, has tollgates, is visibly displayed, is well communicated and is clear to all stakeholders. When leading integration work, thought leaders must have a good process that meets these requirements. The worst thing that can happen is for integration work to begin before stakeholders understand the process, how they fit and the final destination. A good process will reduce integration risk while a bad or absent one is a high-risk proposition.

Finally, once leaders have planned for people, structure and process, the outcomes will come. As noted, the intended outcomes of integration work are people accomplishing more together, economies of scale, growth and competitive advantages gained from the combined operating structure. Putting the cart before the horse will only ensure desired outcomes will never be attained.

CASE STUDY

Let's take a closer look at a real-world integration scenario and its associated risk. A large service organization had been a high performer and industry leader for years. Due to a variety of factors, over time the organization's operational outcomes declined. In short, inefficiencies and waste increased operating costs, impeded service and hampered the quality of services provided. These unfavorable attributes resulted in tens of millions of dollars in waste over a short period of time.

Consequently, the organization was forced to join a larger organization. The end goal was to reduce costs, improve service levels, achieve operational economies of scale and grow market presence. The combination subsequently spawned a litany of integration work. Some of the integration activities were greatly successful while others were not.

A large division began its integration journey by combining five large programs. One of the programs was very well run and structured. It was the 'north star' of the group as it exceeded operational goals, was very nimble and was able to do more with fewer resources as compared to its peers. Unfortunately, the other areas were challenged.

The other programs lacked goal attainment and structurally were not aligned with the market. Subsequently, they were highly disruptive to the organization and its stakeholders. The goal of the integration was to pull all programs together and make them all shining stars. The integration was well intended, but poorly executed.

The enterprise rolled the highly performing group under the other four lesser performing programs. The higher performing group had a balanced talent portfolio. This group was led by an accomplished and nationally recognized thought leader. Also, the team was led operationally by a few leaders that managed the day-to-day operations very well. The group also contained tactical level staff that were tenured, higher performers and champions of the organization's culture. In short, the shining star was cohesive, produced synergy and sustained successes from many years' running.

In contrast, the other groups had limited talent portfolios. Here, none of the groups had a strategic thought leader. All the groups had limited operational leadership that produced outcomes below industry benchmarks. Also, cohesiveness, synergy and successes were nonexistent.

When the integration process began, an operational leader with no strategic prowess was chosen to lead the charge forward. Almost immediately, dysfunction began. The shining star group lost its cohesiveness and synergy. Operational outcomes began to wax and wane. The top performing strategic thought leader was rolled under a less knowledgeable operational leader and the integration work came to a screeching halt.

On one occasion, a draft organizational chart was shared with various stakeholders. Unfortunately, the chart was missing current roles which created a knee jerk reaction by some stakeholders who began to fear for their basic needs (refer to Maslow's Hierarchy of Needs). Simply put, their roles were missing on the integrated structure and the leaders were not aware of the omissions before disseminating the future state structure.

The integration leaders had to immediately regress and reconfigure the structure. As a result, trust was lost and the integration achieved only limited success at best. A thought leader was engaged to repair the integration team and a risk assessment ensued. (See Figure 3.4 for details.)

The thought leader used a simple risk tool that scored each integration team on several factors: scope, impact potential, operating environment, sponsorship, culture and available talent. Ideally, integration teams would possess a stable operating environment, a proactive sponsor, a change driven culture and a balanced talent portfolio consisting of strategic,

Integration	Sponsorship 1-Disengaged 2-Neutral 3-Proactive	Operating Environment 1-Unstable 2-Stable	Impact Potential 1-Life/Safety 2-Mission 3-Important	Culture 1-Change Resistant 2-Neutral 3-Change Acceptant	Available Talent 1-Tactical 2-Operations 3-Strategic	Integration Scope 1-Enterprise Wide 2-Division 3-Department	Risk Score *Sum Columns 2-7 Lower Score = Higher Risk	Risk Level
Integration 1	1	1	1	1	1	3	8	High Risk
Integration 2	2	2	2	2	2	1	11	High Risk
Integration 3	1	1	1	1	3	1	6	High Risk
Integration 4	2	2	2	2	3	1	12	Proceed with Caution
Integration 5	3	2	1	3	3	1	13	Low Risk
Avg Score	1.8	1.6	1.4	1.8	2.0	1.4		
Risk Level	High Risk	High Risk	High Risk	High Risk	Low Risk	High Risk		

FIGURE 3.4

Integration risk tool.

operational and tactical talent. As noted in Figure 3.4, three of the five groups were high risk.

These groups were high risk due to their impact and scope. Their business models were mainly enterprise focused and they impacted mostly life, safety and the organization's mission. To say the least, these programs were vital to the organization's core business. Also, they lacked proactive integration sponsorship and were not culturally aligned for change. Thus, they were simply not ready or primed for integration. Consequently, these groups were disrupted by risk.

As noted in Figure 3.4, only one group was low risk and ready for integration. This was the shining star. Here, the team had proactive sponsorship, a stable operating environment and an aligned change culture. All these positive attributes existed in spite of this team's scope and impact potential being high. Simply put, this program was well run, properly structured and primed for the integration journey.

The other team (Team 4 in Figure 3.4) was an average risk for integration. This team was in a stable operating environment with neutral sponsorship. Also, the team had a moderate impact potential to life, safety and mission. A positive attribute worth noting was the presence of strategic leadership. In short, leadership should have proceeded with caution as average risk was the norm here.

LESSONS LEARNED

So, what did we learn from the case study? One, integration work is a risky business. But, how would one know the risk level if it's not measured? In short, they won't. The lesson here is that leaders don't know what they don't measure. Ignorance is never bliss. Leaders must measure twice and cut once (operationally speaking) to succeed in integration work.

Two, combining teams, departments or organizations does not always work flawlessly. A formula for success is needed to succeed in integration. As noted in the case study, change agents must always begin with people. Put yourself in the shoes of those being affected by the integration changes. It's imperative for leaders to know the answers to basic questions: Where do I fit? Who do I report to? How can/will I contribute to success? Will I have a job? If thought leaders cannot answer these considerations for each stakeholder, then the environment is not ready for integration.

Three, culture is not the only risk factor to consider when bringing teams together. As noted and discussed in detail, other risk factors such as scope, impact potential, operating environment, sponsorship and available talent will determine if integration work succeeds or fails. Thus, thought leaders must view integration through multiple lenses. Otherwise, risk will disrupt the road ahead and result in integration failure.

SUMMARY

In practical terms, integration is a flashy strategy term often over simplified. Bringing people, operations and organizations together is not for the faint-hearted or ill-prepared leaders. There are many pitfalls that integration leaders must avoid. These pitfalls include, but are not limited to, assigning operational leaders to strategic initiatives, not understanding the current state operating environment, failing to plan for all stakeholders, structurally rolling well performing areas under lower performing groups, not utilizing existing talent to their full potential and not being able to answer basic stakeholder questions before the integration process begins.

Looking back, integration is a risky proposition. There are advantages of bringing people groups together if done properly. But, there are also visible and unassuming risks that must be considered. At the end of the day, people simply want to know where they fit, whom they report to and how they contribute to the organization's success.

The key to success is for leaders to understand, measure and mitigate risks before the integration process begins. Effective integration leaders are those that understand and empathize with people, have an effective structure, lead an efficient process and reach the desired end together with others.

REFERENCES

1. Merriam-Webster, 2022.
2. Institute of Industrial and Systems Engineers (IISE), Lean Green Belt, 2016.

4

The Unintended Consequences
of Sharing Knowledge

KNOWLEDGE DEFINED

Knowledge can be defined as, 'information, understanding, or skill that you get from experience or education' (1). Knowledge is synonymous with virtues such as discernment, knowing, insight, wisdom, learning and the like. The key is that knowledge requires action and involves time. With time, people learn and grow in understanding. Thus, they become more knowledgeable.

Knowledge is a strong commodity and should never be underestimated. This concept has been a focal point of leaders for thousands of years. Hosea wrote, 'My people are destroyed for a lack of knowledge' (Hosea 4:6 KJV). King Solomon who is often cited as the wisest person to ever live also focused heavily on knowledge. In Ecclesiastes 7:19, he wrote that, 'Wisdom makes a wise man more powerful than ten rulers in a city.' In Proverbs 12:23, Solomon also took a different perspective on knowledge as it relates to sharing. He advised, 'A wise man keeps his knowledge to himself.'

KNOWLEDGE SHARING SPHERES

There are several levels or spheres of knowledge leaders must consider. (See Figure 4.1 for details.)

Leaders often share knowledge with their inner circle. The inner circle typically is a small group of trusted stakeholders that have influence with and the respect of the leader. The goal here is to create awareness by sharing knowledge. This awareness may range from updates on industry best practices

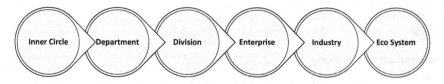

FIGURE 4.1
Knowledge sharing spheres.

or team successes to proprietary details of new concepts or models internally developed.

Departmental level knowledge sharing typically occurs when a department leader shares knowledge with their department. Here, leaders may also share updates or best practices to help the department perform better. Common tactics may include coaching, training, orientation, presentations and the like.

Divisional level knowledge sharing involves multiple departments grouped under a single umbrella. Divisional leaders may often share knowledge on strategic imperatives, industry direction and other high level operational attributes. Regardless of technique, the key is to ensure stakeholders in the division understand and relate to the knowledge being shared. Otherwise, knowledge may be shared but not transferred and utilized for benefit.

Enterprise knowledge sharing involves the entire organization. Typically, this level of sharing originates with top leaders. These leaders may share knowledge related to organizational goals, new strategic initiatives, growth plans, compensation updates that affect all stakeholders, organizational performance outcomes or lack thereof and the like. The takeaway is that enterprise knowledge sharing involves more people, is higher risk and must be planned meticulously.

The final two knowledge sharing spheres are industry level and ecosystem. Industry level sharing is exactly as it sounds. Here, leaders share their organizational or personal knowledge with industry peers. This knowledge transfer may take the form of published outcomes, best practices and other operational insights. The goal is to share knowledge that will help others across the industry perform better. Ecosystem knowledge sharing involves the transfer of knowledge outside of the specific industry. This is the biggest test of sharing knowledge. If other industries find value in your work, it's a testament to the quality of knowledge involved.

CONSEQUENCES OF SHARING KNOWLEDGE

When leaders share knowledge, they must realize that pros and cons exist. The lesson learned is that there are intended and unintended consequences of possessing, cultivating and sharing knowledge. There are several intended consequences of sharing knowledge worth noting. One, leaders share knowledge to simply share knowledge. Here, the goal is to share original content, best practices or lessons learned to help others perform better. The end game is to help others know more, perform better and utilize knowledge to impact humanity positively.

Two, leaders share knowledge in hopes of impacting the industry body of knowledge. Here, leaders share their insights and best practices in various forms. Industry knowledge sharing typically occurs in published articles, presentations at industry venues and the like. The goal is to use insights and knowledge gained to make the industry better. Again, regardless of industry, the measure of success is leveraging knowledge to meet and exceed customer requirements by the most efficient means possible.

A third intended consequence of sharing knowledge is to grow the pie for others. Leaders may share knowledge with colleagues or subordinates, for example, so they can achieve a promotion. Here, knowledge sharing is more selfless with the intent to better the careers of others. Also, growing the pie may entail sharing insights so others perform better and meet more goals. This in turn will help the organization perform better as a whole. The key takeaway is that growing the pie is more about benefiting others with one's knowledge versus self-promotion.

Four, leaders may intend for knowledge sharing to standardize work and subsequent outcomes. In healthcare, for example, standard work is a critical function. If thousands of patients arrive to an emergency room annually suffering a heart attack, variation of care can and will result in significant harm and in some instances may make it worse. Sharing knowledge to standardize work ensures there is a standard process so work is done correctly and in the same way each and every time.

As standardization occurs, outcomes are better and more consistent. Also, value added to stakeholders including customers grows. Value often refers to quality, cost and service levels. The end goal is to maximize value for each customer at every touch point with the organization.

Another intended consequence of sharing knowledge is creating a talent pipeline. Here, organizational leaders focus on succession planning with leadership and other critical roles. A general rule of thumb is to have a primary and backup person trained for each critical role in the organization. Common techniques for depth in roles may include paired work, cross training, shadowing, mentoring, coaching programs, creating job aides or quick guides and the like. The end goal is to ensure the organization has a talent pipeline that knows how the work is done, does the work the same way each time and can sustain success long term regardless of who is leading the enterprise.

Finally, leaders may intend for their knowledge sharing activities to create a legacy of knowledge they leave behind post retirement. Here, leaders focus heavily on creating a body of work consisting of best practices, successes, innovative concepts and improvements that are transferable outside their organization. The end goal is to share what was learned so others can replicate those successes externally and in some instances in other industries.

In contrast, when leaders share knowledge there are also unintended consequences. There is always a risk that knowledge may not be used for the best purposes. Often, leaders find themselves victims of knowledge manipulation. Here, knowledge shared may be used by others to gain credit for work in which they do not own. Sadly, this is a common tactic for leaders that lack original content or may find themselves in roles that they are not equipped to handle.

Another unintended consequence of sharing knowledge is unhealthy competition. This too is an unfortunate aspect of sharing one's knowledge. In certain instances, leaders may find themselves competing with peers who are insecure or fearful of the knowledge that is being shared. This unhealthy competitive spirit results when other leaders attempt to use another leader's knowledge to get promoted or positioned ahead of the leader that produced the original content. Irrespective of the motive, leaders must realize that sharing knowledge is a risky business. Although well intentioned, not all knowledge will achieve the intended outcomes.

KNOWLEDGE SHARING ARCHETYPES

As noted in Figure 4.2, there are three archetypes worth noting.

The first is knowledge bearers. These leaders tend to possess large caches of organizational and industry knowledge. Industry dependent, their knowledge encompasses technical, operational and change management

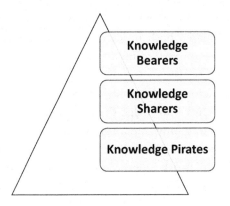

FIGURE 4.2
Knowledge sharing archetypes.

attributes. The adage 'universal soldier' applies here as these leaders have knowledge applicable to all facets of the organization's operating landscape.

The second archetype relates to knowledge sharers. These leaders not only possess high levels of knowledge but also share it. This content may include industry best practices, new models or concepts, original content created by the leader and other innovative insights. These leaders typically are deemed as industry experts who have amassed respectable bodies of work respected and valued by industry peers.

The third archetype is often associated with unintended consequences of sharing knowledge as previously noted. This archetype is represented by the knowledge pirates. These leaders tend to take more than they give or share. They have limited knowledge and often are associated with being opportunists. They regularly repurpose the work of others and leverage outside knowledge for their own benefit even when they didn't create it.

The key is for knowledge sharing leaders to understand their surroundings, the risk of sharing and ensure they align with knowledge bearers and other sharers. It's crucial to also avoid the knowledge pirates. Knowledge is a powerful tool that can help many if leveraged properly. But, knowledge is very dangerous and risky if weaponized by the wrong archetype.

KNOWLEDGE SHARING RISK FACTORS

As noted, sharing knowledge is laden with risk. The first risk factor related to sharing knowledge is the scope. The scope applies to the extent to which knowledge is shared. Will knowledge be shared outside the organization? Will knowledge be shared both inside and outside the organization? Will knowledge sharing be confined to inside the organization only? The broader the scope, the higher the risk.

The second risk factor worth noting is impact potential. Here, leaders must consider the impact knowledge sharing has on life, safety, health and mission. Will the sharing only impact the organization's mission? If so, it's correlated with moderate risk. Will the sharing impact life, safety and health of others? If so, it's a high-risk proposition. If the knowledge being shared is important but does not impact life, safety, health or mission, then it's a low-risk proposition.

The next risk factor for sharing knowledge is culture. Is the organization's culture knowledge abundant? Simply put, are leaders proactively engaged in sharing knowledge, publishing best practices, creating innovative ways of doing business and the like? If so, a learning culture exists and the risk of sharing knowledge is lower. If the culture is knowledge lacking and does not proactively engage in knowledge sharing at the highest levels, then the risks are higher.

Another risk factor worth noting is the operating environment. There are two simple questions leaders must answer. One, is the operating environment stable? Simply put, can leaders meet goals, improve as needed and meet industry benchmarks freely? If the answer is yes, then the risk is low and the operating environment is stable. Two, is the operating environment unstable or out of control? Evidence for this operating state may include significant and prolonged non-goal attainment for major KPIs (key performance indicators), lack of improvement and the inability to perform up to industry benchmarks. Here, the risk of sharing knowledge is very high and caution is warranted.

The fifth risk factor leaders must consider for sharing knowledge is trust levels. Trust correlates back to group or environmental factors. Trust occurs when everyone contributes to success and everyone focuses on excellence. If trust is plentiful, then the risk is lower. If the leader sharing is the only one contributing to success, then trust is low and risk is high.

The final risk factor of knowledge sharing relates to the value proposition. Does the organization value knowledge sharing? Simply put, if leaders share their knowledge to help others and the organization, will their brand, value and rewards increase? If the answer to all of the above is yes, then risk is low and value is high. If leaders are not rewarded or value for sharing knowledge, then value is lacking and risk of doing so is higher than desired. Thus, leaders must ensure their insights and best practices are valued. Otherwise, the knowledge pirates will raid the cache.

KNOWLEDGE SHARING COUNTER MEASURES

To ensure one's knowledge is maximized and not exploited, leaders should consider several proactive counter measures. The end goal in sharing knowledge is to ensure the intended consequences of growing the pie, positively impacting humanity, maximizing value and the like are realized. The first guardrail needed is a risk assessment. (See Figure 4.3 for details.)

In Figure 4.3, there are six attributes leaders should risk assess before sharing knowledge. The attributes include trust levels, operating environment, impact potential, culture, value proposition and the scope of knowledge sharing. These attributes were discussed previously in detail. As noted, there are four scenarios or knowledge sharing opportunities for leadership consideration.

Two of the opportunities are high risk. Here, trust is low and the operating environment is stable. Also, sharing knowledge is not valued as expected and the culture is not aligned. Thus, leaders should avoid these high-risk opportunities.

Scenario 4 is low risk. The risk is low because the environment is stable, the trust levels are higher and culture is aligned to value knowledge sharing. Simply put, it's a safer environment because more higher performing leaders are present in the form of knowledge bearers and sharers. Also, the risk of encountering a knowledge pirate is much lower. Thus, leaders should feel comfortable sharing knowledge in this environment.

Scenario 2, as noted in the figure, is average risk. Here, trust and operating stability are marginal at best. Also, the organization rewards and values sharing knowledge. Moreover, the culture is aligned with an abundance of knowledge (i.e., knowledge bearers and sharers). But, the impact and scope are very risky. Thus, leaders should proceed with caution and only share knowledge here if no other low-risk opportunities exist.

The key from the risk tool is for leaders to choose sharing opportunities wisely. The lower the risk, the better the venue or opportunity. At all costs, leaders should avoid high-risk knowledge sharing venues.

Scenario	Trust Levels 1-Low 2-Medium 3-High	Operating Environment 1-Unstable 2-Stable	Impact Potential 1-Life/Safety 2-Mission 3-Important	Culture 1-Knowledge Lacking 2-Knowledge Abundant	Knowledge Value Proposition 1-Not Valued 2-Rewarded 3-Rewarded + Valued	Knowledge Scope 1-External Sharing 2-External + Internal Sharing 3-Internal Sharing	Risk Score *Sum Columns 2-7 Lower Score = Higher Risk	Risk Level
Scenario 1	1	1	1	1	1	1	6	High Risk
Scenario 2	2	2	2	2	2	1	11	Average Risk
Scenario 3	1	1	1	1	1	1	6	High Risk
Scenario 4	3	2	2	2	3	1	13	Low Risk
Avg Score	1.8	1.5	1.5	1.5	1.8	1.0		
Risk Level	High Risk	High Risk	High Risk	High Risk	High Risk	High Risk		

FIGURE 4.3

Knowledge sharing risk tool.

The second counter measure for knowledge sharing is to share wisely. One common technique is to only share published work with stakeholders, colleagues and other peers. Once copyrighted, others will not be able to readily use the body of knowledge freely or gain credit for work that is not warranted. The key here is to not let the cat out of the bag prematurely. Although knowledge can be exciting and naïve leaders desire to share it, wise leaders, as Solomon wrote, often keep their knowledge to themselves until the right venue presents itself.

The third and final counter measure for knowledge sharing is to hold original content close to the vest. Simply put, effective leaders will be expected and called upon to solve problems, create innovative solutions and share knowledge. But, you don't have to 'give away the farm' in the process. If you create original content, a simple tactic is not to share editable documents. Also, when sharing before risk is determined or the work is copyrighted it's a good rule of thumb to share surface level knowledge only. Keep the details for the appropriate venue where risk is lower.

SUMMARY

Sharing knowledge is a risky proposition. Although intentions of sharing insights and best practices may be noble, there are both intended and unintended consequences that leaders must consider. The keys to success in sharing insights are for leaders to understand the environment, leverage trust filled relationships, mitigate risks, align cultures and ensure the organization values the knowledge contributions.

Effective leaders are those that align with knowledge bearers and sharers, avoid pirates and grow the pie for others. As noted, without knowledge teams and organizations perish. Moreover, leaders don't know what they don't measure. Risk is prevalent and a common denominator in knowledge sharing. Thus, leaders that wisely share knowledge will eliminate unintended consequences (i.e., risks) and reap a harvest of insight that favorably impacts humanity for generations to come.

REFERENCE

1. Merriam-Webster, 2022.

5

The Side Winder Effect: When Leaders Misinterpret Root Causes of Success

SUCCESS DEFINED

Is all success true success or a simple mirage that doesn't last? Can success be measured over time? Is it possible for leaders to misinterpret the root causes of success? Is a simple improvement in a metric a true success? Can leaders disrupt high performing teams by not understanding the root causes of success and make disruptive changes that are not warranted? Is an improved metric the ultimate signal of success or is sustaining team synergy long term the ideal threshold? Can all leaders attain breakthrough transformational success or is a special skill set required? We will answer these considerations and more in the following.

Success can be defined as 'the accomplishment of one's goals' (1). This concept is often synonymous with achievement, fame, fortune, goal attainment and the like. But, is accomplishing a goal really the best measure of success? Arguably, goal attainment is part of the success process, but there is more needed.

THE PROCESS

Success is a process, not a destination. (See Figure 5.1 for details.)

The process begins with leaders identifying a target or focal point. The target of success may vary from one industry to another. Some leaders may target the value equation for example. This simply consists of service, cost and quality which are common to all industries. Ideally, the target should

DOI: 10.4324/9781003439127-5

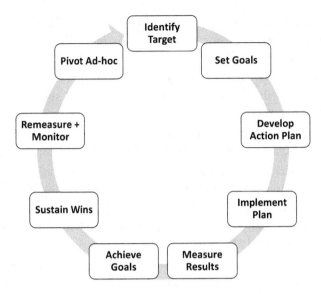

FIGURE 5.1
Success process.

be aligned with customer requirements as value is anything a customer is willing to pay for (2).

Next, the focus shifts to goals. Here, success is partly defined. The most important question leaders will be asked on the success journey is, 'What is success?' This is where goals come into play. Goals are the tollgates along the journey or desired end.

It's imperative for leaders to define their goals and ensure they are attainable. For example, a goal to 'improve quality of services' is not adequate. What's the success threshold here? Over what time period will quality be improved? A more functional goal tied to improving quality of services can mirror the following. The goal is to improve the quality metric 'x' by 30% within six months. The key is that this goal statement has a defined target, an improvement threshold of 30% and a time component.

Once goals are defined and agreed to, leaders must then develop action plans that will lead to goal attainment. Plans also need to be well defined, aligned with the current state, have a start and stop date, and have responsibility assigned to the appropriate leadership. Again, just as vague goals are not effective, so are vague plans. Simply put, the plan(s) should outline what is to be done, when each item is due and who owns each deliverable.

Next, leaders implement their plans. Implementation is often perceived as a 'no brainer.' But, leaders unfortunately learn the hard way that how plans are implemented can lead to a smooth journey ahead or derail the train. It's imperative for leaders to ensure implementation has a schedule, tollgates for each phase of the journey and are measurable so progress can be tracked.

Once implemented, leaders should measure the results of their implemented plans. The results should be measurable, verifiable and significant. If not, leaders quickly become heroes in their own minds. To measure success, in this perspective, there are three basic questions to answer. One, did we meet the goal(s)? Two, did we improve the goal if the goal was not met? Three, is the outcomes data in or out of control? This final consideration will require additional skill and insight to leverage control charts. But, the key is for leaders to measure data, test it and ensure the improvement(s) are significant.

If goals are not met, the leaders should pivot and reassess the situation before moving forward. Without goal attainment, the success train stops. If goals are met, the team should move on to sustaining those wins. This is arguably one of the most crucial and difficult steps in the success process. Here, leaders will have their metal tested. Once stakeholders shift their attention away from the initiative, leaders must work diligently to ensure progress is not lost.

Once leaders determine that goals are achieved and sustained, frequent remeasurement occurs. The frequency of remeasuring outcome data and the process depend on the environment, focal point and culture of the initiative. The goal is to ensure the wins or gains stand the test of time. If retrenchment occurs, leaders must pivot quickly to ensure they regain the wins before it's too late and recovery is not feasible.

SUCCESS MATRIX

To accompany the process as noted in Figure 5.1, leaders may also find a simple rule of thumb helpful in determining if an initiative was or is successful. (See Figure 5.2 for details.)

As noted in the figure, there are two attributes: level of success and duration. The level of success can be simply described as high or low. But, leaders must use quantitative measurements to validate either assertion.

Here is a simple example. A team sets a goal to reduce hospital infection rates by 30% in three months. The team realizes 60% reductions in infection rates by the timeline prescribed. This can be considered a high level of success.

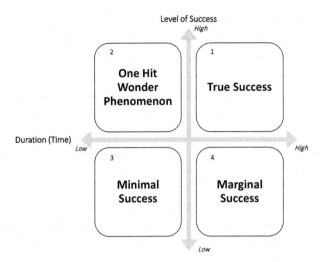

FIGURE 5.2
Success matrix.

The thresholds will depend upon the organization, its needs and market or benchmark data.

In contrast, if the team sets the same goal for hospital infection rates and only reduces the metric by .5%, then this is a low level of success. The level of success is directly dependent upon the quantitative outcome based on the prescribed goal.

The second attribute in Figure 5.2 is duration or time. Ideally, all wins or success will be sustained indefinitely. But, that is unfortunately not always the case. The rating here is also high or low. Leaders will again need to assign a quantitative measure to each outcome attribute. Let's revisit the hospital infection rate example. If the team sustains its goal for one week, then, duration would be low. If the team sustains significant reductions in infection rates for five years, then this would be high on the duration spectrum.

When using Figure 5.2 as a simple rule of thumb, the goal is for leaders to quickly assess an initiative for success. Those focal points that have high levels of success and are sustained for long periods of time are true successes as noted in box 1. This is the ideal success category for any initiative.

As noted in box 2, initiatives that have a high degree of success but are not sustained can arguably be classified as limited success. The 'one hit wonder' adage may apply here. Some success is better than no success. But, this state is not ideal.

Box 3 is categorized as minimal success. Here, success levels and duration of sustaining wins are both low. Initiatives that fall into this category would not be considered a success. In layman's terms the adage 'waste of time' may apply here.

Box 4 indicates the initiative had low levels of success that were sustained over time. Again, success is relative to the environment, goals and desired end. But, the outcomes here would be considered a marginal success at best. The adage of 'better some success than no success' would be applicable here.

So, what was learned from the success process and matrix? One, success is a process and multidimensional. Also, success is not a destination. Rather it's a process that continues over time. Two, success is not a one size fits all scenario. There are various levels of success based on predetermined goals, customer expectations and operating environments. Moreover, an initial win may not remain in the success category if not sustained over time. The takeaway is that perception is not always reality. What sparkles may not always shine. A success needs to be validated to ensure it meets the threshold.

THE SIDE WINDER EFFECT

Once leaders attain success, one of the biggest tests of their mental states is what they do with it. This leads to a consideration of a side winder rattle snake. When the snake crawls to make forward progress, its track in the sand leaves a pattern with significant ups and downs. Although it appears to be uncoordinated, the snake moves methodically through rough terrain to the final destination.

The same pattern can easily be associated with leadership career journeys. Let's look further at a real example. A thought leader was recognized in the service industry as a turnaround expert or 'fix it' change agent. The leader's organization was experiencing significant challenges in one of its critical business units for several years. The outcomes were directly impacting customers and the value equation (previously noted). In short, if the organization did not correct these issues, its market viability would decline quickly.

The change agent started the journey by using a simple tool noted in Figure 6.3.

Major tollgates over a number of years were listed for the business unit and scored on a scale ranging from operational negative to external positive.

Initiative	Success Rating
Initiative 1	-3
Initiative 2	-3
Initiative 3	-3
Initiative 4	-2
Initiative 5	-1
Initiative 6	-1
Initiative 7	2
Initiative 8	2
Initiative 9	2
Initiative 10	2
Initiative 11	1
Initiative 12	3
Initiative 13	3
Initiative 14	3
Initiative 15	3
Initiative 16	3
Initiative 17	3
Initiative 18	3
Initiative 19	3
Initiative 20	2
Initiative 21	-1
Initiative 22	-3
Initiative 23	-3
Initiative 24	-1

Legend	
Score	Rating
Operational Negative	-1
Organizational Negative	-2
External Negative	-3
Operational Positive	1
Organizational Positive	2
External Positive	3

FIGURE 5.3
Side winder effect scoring legend.

Operational negatives were tollgates that imposed negative outcomes from an operational standpoint. These impacted the business unit itself. Organizational negatives were unfavorable outcomes from tollgates in the business unit that impacted the organization as a whole. The external negative category as noted in Figure 5.3's legend pertained to outcomes produced by the business unit that negatively impacted stakeholders outside the organization. Think of partners, potential partners and the like.

In contrast, there were three positive ratings. Here, the positives impacted the business unit's operational outcomes, the organization as a whole or external stakeholders. The end goal was for the business unit to positively impact the unit itself, the organization and external stakeholders. For years the business unit was grossly underperforming and not successful.

The leader completed an assessment and noted each major tollgate completed by business unit leaders for the time period. The first six were negative ranging from operational negatives to external negatives. Needless to say, these outcomes were not ideal and warranted a structural change.

The thought leader led a restructure and turnaround of the business unit. Shortly after, the outcomes shifted from negative to positive as noted in the figure. For tollgates seven through twenty, the business unit's outcomes were overwhelmingly positive for years and greatly impacted many stakeholders externally. These outcomes and many other quantitative metrics proved that the revised structure, process and outcomes were significant. Thus, success became the operating norm.

As time passed, the team became comfortable with success and even realized national recognition for its journey. The team grew and so did some unfavorable attributes. At tollgate 21, as noted in the figure, the business unit's team dynamic shifted. Some leaders took success for granted and wanted more of it. Self-interests, ego and self-ambition began to grow. Leaders began lane jumping and strayed away from their core skill sets to compete with other business unit leaders with different strengths. Their goal was to be seen, heard and grow their roles at any cost.

These trends unraveled the team dynamic. As time passed, this behavior accelerated and synergies or wins began to decline as trust, mutual respect and the team structure deteriorated. The business unit transitioned from an impenetrable fortress (operationally speaking) to a piece of Swiss cheese. Negative patterns of old quickly reappeared.

Eventually, some of the overzealous leaders maneuvered a takeover of sorts. When this occurred, the business unit was restructured again as noted in Figure 5.4.

This time the restructure was unwarranted and did not make good operational sense. The adage of 'if it ain't broke, don't fix it' applies here.

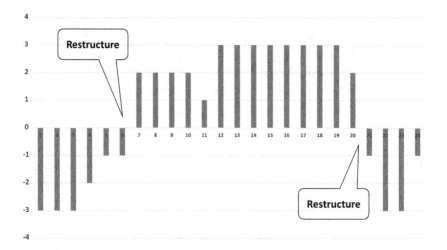

FIGURE 5.4
Side winder effect chart.

As soon as the restructure occurred, the outcomes flipped back to negative. Thus, the side winder effect appeared. When significant leadership dysfunction was present, operational negatives were the norm. When effective leadership was in control, greatly positive outcomes were commonplace. This begs the question: Why was change implemented when it was not warranted?

Back to the success focus, Figure 5.4 is a very simple depiction of how leaders can ruin a successful team by not understanding the root causes of success. The business unit's successes were directly attributed to several conditions. One, leaders establish a cohesive work environment where trust was the norm and expectation of each team member. The trust foci included everyone contributing to success, excellence being the norm and a safe place for the team to succeed and fail. As leaders became over competitive with one another seeking self-promotion, trust was lost and cohesiveness followed suit.

Two, the team was successful because of synergies. Here, the team and its leaders simply focused on their 'bread and butter' skill sets. Everyone mastered their strengths which covered the weaknesses of others. When leaders began lane jumping into areas in which they were not as strong, mistakes occurred and the business unit's outcomes floundered.

Three, the team as a whole was successful due to a team spirit that celebrated everyone's wins regardless of whose name was on the billboard. The success of one or a limited number of leaders was a win for the team. As internal competition increased among the leaders, the team spirit faded into defensive postures and self-preservation. Thus, outcomes declined.

The takeaway is that the leaders misinterpreted the root causes of success. Success was predicated on and thrived in a solidified environment built on trust. Also, when leaders celebrated each other versus when they competed with each other, success was greatly abundant. Simply put, the team accomplished more together than apart. As noted in Mark 3:25 NIV, a house divided cannot stand. As division occurred, success became marginal at best and what appeared to be a success was simply not.

SUMMARY

In review, success is not as simple as it seems. Success is multifactorial and complicated. For leaders to claim a success exists, there must be a process, measurable outcomes, goal attainment and sustained wins. If not, perceived success is simply a mirage in the desert that disappears quickly.

But, how will leaders understand success if they don't measure it? Simply put, they won't. The fact is that perception is not always reality. Ignorance is never bliss. What leaders and their organizations don't know will eventually unfavorably impact them and their customers.

The reality is that leaders can prevent success or disrupt successful teams and operations if they misinterpret the root causes of success. When self-interests and ego override the team spirit, the side winder effect appears. The keys to success are building cohesive teams, cultivating trust, winning together, measuring outcomes, validating wins and having a good process. Success in the simplest of terms is not just meeting a goal. It's leading people along a journey, achieving goals at each milestone, celebrating the success of others and sustaining wins long term. Anything short of that is simply not a success.

REFERENCES

1. www.Dictionary.com, 2022.
2. Institute of Industrial and Systems Engineers (IISE), Lean Green Belt, 2016.

6

The Leadership Test of Humility

HUMILITY DEFINED

Humility can be defined as 'the quality or state of not thinking you are better than other people' (1). In layman's terms, humility from a leadership standpoint is being able to harness power, control, knowledge, insight and success to benefit others. Years ago, a top thought leader engaged a younger rising star leader. The more senior leader told the protégé, 'You have all the answers to problems that people need, you're wise beyond your years, but you lack humility.' The protégé was so naïve that they did not understand the implication. After many years and several tests of humility, the protégé realized that leadership was not about power, control or success. Leadership is a privilege entrusted to some for the betterment of others.

This concept begs several considerations. Is humility a choice or a naturally occurring phenomenon embedded in the DNA of leaders? Will all leaders experience a test of humility along the career journey? Can leaders sustain success without humility? Can pride or ego end one's career prematurely? Can humility accelerate leadership growth, success and opportunities? We will answer these and other considerations in the following.

LEADERSHIP DIMENSIONS

There are several leadership dimensions worth noting. (See Figure 6.1 for details.)

These dimensions are required elements for leaders to succeed. But, if the proportion of the attributes becomes skewed, problems will arise. The

DOI: 10.4324/9781003439127-6

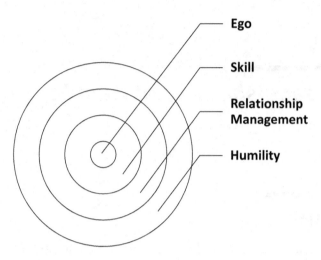

Ego

Skill

Relationship Management

Humility

FIGURE 6.1
Leadership dimensions.

first dimension of leadership is ego. Ego has both healthy and unhealthy connotations. In the simplest of terms, one's healthy ego is synonymous with self-perception, self-regard, self-esteem or self-image. (1) Here, leaders need a healthy dose of confidence in their abilities to make decisions, lead others and solve problems.

In contrast, ego can easily become unhealthy when these attributes are inflated. In this case, ego is associated with pride. In Proverbs (16:18 KJV) it is written that 'Pride goes before destruction and a haughty spirit before a fall.' Simply put, a healthy dose of ego is needed for leaders to succeed while unhealthy ego or pride will always result in a test of humility.

The second leadership dimension is skill. Here leaders must have basic skills, knowledge and abilities to succeed. Leadership skill is mainly dependent upon the industry and role. But, it is a basic rule of thumb that is applicable to leadership regardless of industry. In today's world, change is the new norm and only constant. With change comes risk. The more change that exists, the riskier the operating environment for leadership.

Thus, leaders need three basic skills. The first is technical skills. Industry dependent, leaders must understand their business and be proficient in completing the basic work. Technical skills are often synonymous with tactical skills.

Second, leaders need operational skills. Here, leaders garner and cultivate skill to lead people, make decisions that impact others and solve problems.

This skill comes with time, trial and error. The adage of 'the school of hard knocks' applies here.

Third, leaders really need improvement or change agent skills in high-risk environments. Often, leaders may choose training in methodologies included, but not limited to, Lean, Six Sigma and the like. Irrespective of the methodology, leaders must be able to implement change, align organizational culture to change, measure its outcomes and pivot as indicated. There is nothing worse as a leader than not knowing what needs to be done, when it needs to be done or how to do what is needed.

The third leadership dimension is relationship management. Leadership is a people business. Thus, leaders must understand people, empathize with them and be able to manage interactions. But, what constitutes a relationship? Should leaders only focus on managing relationships with friends or coworkers? Should they focus mainly on managing relationships with their primary customer (industry dependent)? The simplest answer is no.

Leaders must know who their customers or stakeholders are and what they want. Relationship management for leaders encompasses all stakeholders both internal and external. These stakeholders may include colleagues, partners, potential partners, regulatory bodies, governmental agencies, direct customers, communities, staff, peers, leaders, board members and so many more too numerous to mention. The key is for leaders to create an exhaustive list of all stakeholders, understand what they want and cultivate those relationships so value is added to all.

One of the biggest pitfalls for leaders is to mistake politics for relationship management. In layman's terms, politics is leveraging relationships to get what one wants. Here, leaders often fail by promising to give stakeholders what they want. Often, the promise or deliverable may not be in the best interest of others. In contrast, relationship management is an integrity driven approach to understand stakeholders, empathize with their needs and produce the right deliverables for everyone involved. Not a short-sighted view to meet the needs of a few political contacts.

The fourth dimension of leadership is humility. As previously noted, leaders must actively pursue a humble persona. Humility does not always come automatically and is not built into the DNA of all leaders. As leaders grow in wisdom, knowledge and success, the need for humility becomes a significant priority.

As noted in Figure 6.1, it's imperative for leaders to keep a healthy proportion of all attributes. As indicated, the amount of humility required for success eclipses all other attributes. If ego is greater than humility, then the leader will involuntarily be enrolled in a 'woodshed' experience to tame their pride. Thus, ego must be the smallest dimension of the leadership persona. Also, the ability to manage relationships will often overshadow basic skill sets. The key is that leaders need and must have all four dimensions, but a healthy proportion is required to achieve and sustain success long term.

THE TEST OF HUMILITY

So, what is a test of humility? Often, leaders jokingly refer to a test of humility as the 'woodshed' experience. In talking to older generations, they humorously tell stories of their childhood when they were taken to the woodshed and disciplined for bad behavior. This concept is also applicable to leadership in today's operating environment. Although the woodshed may not be a physical place leaders are sent to receive physical discipline, it's a real experience that dispenses a test to address ego and pride.

Test of Humility Drivers

There are several reasons leaders may be sent (theoretically) to the leadership woodshed. One test of humility may be due to pride or ego. As previously noted, often leaders fall to pride or ego as they grow along the career journey. Success, attention and notoriety can be addicting and to be honest they feel good to leaders. If ego becomes unharnessed, it turns into pride and the next step is a trip to the woodshed.

Another driver for a leadership test of humility may be self-ambition. Here, leaders become consumed with their success, notoriety, accolades and the material gains associated. When this occurs, leaders often experience a 'loss of calling.' At the end of the day, leadership is a calling with the intent of helping others. When leaders forget this basic premise, a trip to the woodshed may be in order.

Third, leaders often face a test of humility due to self-promotion. Self-promotion is a slippery slope that can be good in some cases, but detrimental in others. From this perspective, leaders often lack humility when they over promote their abilities, skills and potential to deliver outcomes. The adage of 'over promise and under deliver' applies here. Self-promotion can easily lead to an unhealthy ego and a self-serving leadership platform. Thus, a test of humility may follow.

Another leadership woodshed driver may entail a lack of integrity or unhealthy motives. Integrity is simply doing the right thing whether anyone is watching or not. Integrity is synonymous with character, moral fortitude, honesty, rightness and the like (1). Lacking integrity is directly correlated to one's core values.

These values are operating norms or guardrails of expected behavior for leadership. Any behavior outside these values is a cardinal or major offense. Think of a physician, nurse or paramedic in the healthcare industry. Upon completion of all academic training, these professionals take a pledge to uphold a code of ethics. Essentially, they pledge to use their skills to help others in good conscience and ultimately to do no harm to anyone.

Any violation of this code is a career ender. Leadership is no different. When leaders fail to operate with integrity, have unhealthy motives and serve I instead of us or we, a test of humility often follows. Unfortunately, the love for money, financial gain, control and power over others can blind leaders. Thus, the woodshed experience derails the leadership journey.

Leadership Test of Humility Reactions

As leaders are involuntarily enrolled in a test of humility, there are several common reactions. One, leaders may voluntarily humble themselves and submit to correction. Unfortunately, this reaction is often not the norm. Most leaders don't self-correct and need an external helping hand. Here, the leadership moral compass and conscience guide the leader back to the center or a place of humility.

Another leadership reaction to the woodshed experience may be fear and anxiety. The main question asked here is why? Why am I being chastised for performing well? Why am I being corrected when I'm producing results? Why are peers and senior leaders not valuing my contributions? See the common theme? The focus tends to shift to I or me.

A third reaction may entail anger or resistance. Think of the body's natural fight or flight response. Here, leaders invest massive amounts of energy to fight corrections. Often, these candidates in the school of humility are blinded by ego or pride. The adage of 'I can do no wrong' is the common theme. These leaders feel correction is unwarranted and fight any attempt by outside influences to change their behavior or operating norms.

A final response from leaders experiencing a test of humility may be flight. Here, leaders try to run from or avoid the woodshed. Common tactics may be to play politics, look for political cover from allies, blame shift to others for issues they own and the like. Irrespectively, leaders fail to see the forest for the trees. In reality, they have lost humility and need a course correction. If not, success will evaporate or be unattainable.

Humility Woodshed Examples

As noted previously, in today's operating landscape leaders are not sent to a woodshed behind the house for discipline. The test of humility may come in various other forms. One, the test may be a demotion. When leaders get their heads over their skies by thinking they are more competent than reality shows, often a demotion occurs as they cannot perform to expected levels. Leaders' pride and ego are checked when responsibility, clout and respect are stripped. This is one of the most painful tests of humility that leaders may experience.

Two, the test may involve a new superior reporting relationship. Leaders may be moved from a covering senior leader that is supportive to one who has no affection for them. Here, the leader's weaknesses or shortcomings may be exposed. A management plan may be the course of action imposed by the new superior. The plan may require the leader to learn new skills, meet more goals, work with other people outside of their comfort zone, perform at higher levels and the like. If the leader concedes their pride, then success may follow. If they resist, the test only gets worse.

Three, the woodshed experience may shift the leader from the inner circle to the periphery. Often, leaders refer to the inner circle as the political 'click.' This click may include a small number of political cronies that work together to achieve an end. In some cases, the end may be a noble cause, and in others, it's not. Irrespectively, the leader may lose their seat at the table with peers or superiors. They may also be pushed out of the room all together. The key is the response. If the leader resists, the test will get worse. If they pass the test of humility by placing their ego in check, recovery is a possibility.

A fourth and often unexpected test of humility is a promotion. Are all promotions ideal? Will a promotion ensure long-term success? Is a promotion the signal of a state of professional bliss? The short answer is not always.

For those leaders that are humble, prepared and ready, a promotion is ideal. The new responsibilities are exciting, challenging and rewarding. For those ego driven leaders that unhealthily self-promote or over promise beyond their capabilities, a promotion is a risky proposition. These leaders often find the promotion to be scary, unmanageable and overwhelming. Unfortunately, a promotion to the wrong leadership archetype can steal joy, peace and quality of life and impact those around them unfavorably. That is why a promotion can easily be masked as a Trojan horse. It looks, seems and feels ideal at first, but in the end it becomes deadly (professionally speaking). Thus, it qualifies as a test of humility.

The final example of a leadership woodshed experience could take the form of a health problem. Here, leaders spend countless hours daily working, striving and manipulating to attain more wealth, power and control. They are so focused on their role and what it can provide to them that they lose their purpose. As time progresses, they negate the basic essentials of good health.

They don't exercise, eat right or get good rest. With time, their health fails and they are forced into the test of humility. Some accept corrections while others resist them. The consequences can range from a minor setback to career ender. Either way, leaders may unintentionally or unknowingly welcome a test of humility by placing achievements over their own physical wellbeing. This begs the question, 'What is really important in life?'

HUMILITY MATRIX

There is a simple rule of thumb leaders can use to test their humility. As noted in Figure 6.2, there are two attributes: lingo and primary driver. Both of these attributes are focused on the leader in question. Lingo refers to what phrases are commonly used by the leader. Is 'I' or 'me' the word of choice or is 'us' or 'we' the lingo?

The primary driver relates to the leader's passion for being in leadership. Is the leader driven by helping others or helping themselves? Is the leader self-interested or is helping others improve and be better a strategic priority? The premise is simple. Does the leader grow the pie for others or are they simply growing the pie for themself?

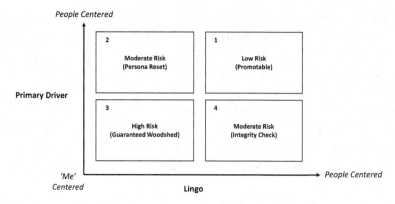

FIGURE 6.2
Leadership humility matrix.

As noted in Figure 6.2, there are four quadrants or boxes. Box 1 represents a low-risk leadership type as it relates to humility. Here, the leader is people centered on both their primary driver of being a leader and their lingo. This leader archetype will commonly use the vocabulary 'we' or 'us' instead of 'I' or 'me.' Thus, the course of action for this leader would be promotion. This is the best-case scenario and an ideal leadership model.

Box 2 in the figure is moderate risk. This leader type is people centered as it relates to their driver for being a leader. The goal is to help others more than self. But, their lingo is more 'me' centered which is not ideal. Thus, the leader needs a persona reset to reduce the risk of a test of humility.

Box 3 represents a high-risk leader. This is the worst-case scenario in terms of humility for a leader. Here, the leader is focused on growing their own pie and constantly uses lingo centered around 'I' or 'me.' In this case, the leader is destined for a woodshed experience. As humility is grossly lacking, the test is just around the corner.

Box 4 is also moderate risk. Leaders in this category use the proper lingo focusing on 'us' or 'we,' but are driven by self-accomplishment. Thus, the risk is higher. These leaders need an integrity check to recenter their operating norms, values and behavior. Otherwise, a test in humility will follow quickly.

The takeaway is that leaders can gauge their risk for a woodshed experience with a simple matrix. Not all leaders have humility ingrained in their DNA. Some leaders are more humble and people centric than others. But, leaders don't know what they don't measure. Also, ignorance is never bliss. If measured and mitigated, leaders can tame their pride or ego and avoid the woodshed.

HUMILITY RISK TOOL

As noted in Figure 6.3, a leadership humility risk tool is also another helpful guide for leaders and organizations to assess their risk of a fall. In the tool, leaders are assessed on several attributes: lingo, primary driver, significant accomplishments, knowledge sharing, legacy plan and strategic perspective. As noted in a previous discussion, lingo and primary driver both relate to the leader's perspective. Is the leader 'I' or 'me' driven versus 'us' or 'we' focused. The more self-interests are the focal point, the greater the risk.

The risk tool also scores each leader on knowledge sharing. Here, leaders are scored as taking more from others than they give, keeping knowledge to themselves or freely sharing what they know. Those leaders that take more or don't share knowledge are higher risk.

Legacy planning is also a risk factor for leadership humility. Does the leader mainly focus on magnifying their persona in the years to come? Does the leader invest their time in impacting the industry body of knowledge to leave a legacy that will benefit others? The premise is simple. Those legacy builders focused on self are higher risk.

Finally, each leader in the tool is scored on their strategic perspective. If a leader was asked to produce their strategic canvas, what would be on it? Would strategic goals for the leader's advancement, success and achievement dominate the canvas? Would the canvas mainly focus on helping others achieve their bucket list goals and improve? Those leaders that are more self-interested strategically are higher risk for a fall and test of humility.

Let's look at Figure 6.3 practically. In the example, four leaders are scored on the attributes previously mentioned. Only one leader is low risk and considered to be promotable. This leader is more people driven than ego focused. Thus, they are ready for next level responsibilities.

Two or 50% of the leaders are high risk and headed for a woodshed experience. These leaders are driven by self-ego, self-ambition and self-promotion. Also, they tend to hold knowledge close to the vest instead of sharing. Moreover, their strategic focus is centered on 'I' or 'me' versus 'others.' Their journey ahead will most definitely include a test of humility.

Only one of the leaders risk scored is average risk. This leader's journey should include an integrity check. Their lingo and primary passion for being a leader are self-absorbed. But, they have invested significantly in helping others accomplish their goals, growing the pie outside the organization and

Leader	Lingo 1-I or Me 2-Us or We	Primary Driver 1-Personal Gain 2-Gain of Others	Significant Accomplishments 1-What You Wanted 2-What Others Needed	Knowledge Sharing 1-Take More Than You Give 2-Keep Knowledge To Yourself 3-Freely Share Knowledge	Legacy Plan 1-Magnify Your Persona 2-Impact Body of Knowledge	Strategic Perspective 1-Focus on Self 2-Focus on Inner Circle 3-Focus on External Stakeholders	Risk Score *Sum Columns 2-7 Lower Score = Higher Risk	Risk Level	Journey Ahead
Leader 1	1	1	1	1	1	1	6	High Risk	Woodshed
Leader 2	2	2	2	2	2	2	12	Low Risk	Promotable
Leader 3	1	1	2	1	2	3	10	Average Risk	Integrity Check
Leader 4	1	1	1	2	2	2	9	High Risk	Woodshed
Avg Score	1.3	1.3	1.5	1.5	1.8	2.0			
Risk Level	High Risk	High Risk	High Risk	High Risk	High Risk	Low Risk			

FIGURE 6.3

Leadership humility risk tool.

impacting the industry body of knowledge. Thus, an integrity check is in order. If not tamed, their self-focus will lead to the woodshed of humility.

The takeaway from the risk tool is that the cohort of leaders is diverse. Seventy-five percent of the leaders are not ready for more power, control or influence. If these leaders are trusted with more, they will eventually fall. Only 25% of the group is promotable. Thus, organizations must choose wisely when allowing people to assume the leadership mantle. Simply put, some leaders can handle the stage and responsibility while others cannot. The adage of 'choose wisely' applies here.

SUMMARY

In retrospect, humility is a required element for leaders to succeed and sustain success long term. But, not all leaders possess the required elements to avoid the woodshed. Humility is a choice that all leaders will wrestle with their entire careers. With success, power and material increase comes the risk of pride, ego and self-absorbed perspectives. The question is how many leaders will ideally avoid the test of humility or make it out of the woodshed unscathed.

The reality is that a lack of or loss of humility can be a career ender. In contrast, humility can accelerate leadership growth, success and opportunities. Effective leaders are those that keep their egos in check, grow the pie for others, know their humility risk and stay out of the woodshed. Do you know your leadership humility risk score? If not, take the test to avoid a fall.

REFERENCE

1. Merriam-Webster, 2022.

7

Leadership Match Making: Finding the Right Leader for the Organization's Problems

Recently, a CEO of a large service organization stated that the number one responsibility as a CEO was to ensure the organization had the right culture. Is this really true? Is the main responsibility of a top leader, regardless of industry, to focus mainly on cultural alignment? Is this a silo approach to leadership? Are there other critical factors that leaders must ensure are present to succeed? Should top leaders have a multi-dimensional approach to success? Can organizations succeed if leaders are not matched to the right problem? We will answer these and other considerations in the following.

THE RIGHT FIT

A thought leader was invited to a large leadership meeting in an auditorium like setting. The thought leader worked for a large service organization. The auditorium was assembled with tables in various rows with seating available for hundreds of leaders. It was first come first serve. Invitees included front-line leaders up to the Executive Suite.

As leaders arrived for the meeting the thought leader sat at the table with a group of peers. There were two seats open. Without notice, a senior leader sat at the head of the table. Minutes before the meeting began, the top leader said, 'We need to find the right fit for this last seat.' Everyone at the table began to ask themselves, 'What does the right fit mean?'

DOI: 10.4324/9781003439127-7

The senior leader began looking around the room at those in attendance. He also began scanning the door for late entrants. Unfortunately, the leader audibly would judge leaders as they walked in as 'not a good fit' or a 'good fit.' Everyone still struggled to understand what made a leader a good fit versus not a good fit.

Was it appearance? Was it reputation? Was it the way someone dressed? Was it personality? Was it likeability? Needless to say, the 'right fit' remained a mystery as this term had been used in senior level leadership circles for years.

The interesting part was the organization had been experiencing an operational decline for several years at this time. Top leaders cycled in and out of the organization with an average tenure of one to two years. As leaders were selected, internally or externally, for these vacant roles organizational announcements would be e-mailed out. The wording was simple: Please welcome leader 'x' to this new role as they are the right fit for this position. There was always a small blurb about credentials. But, most in the organization struggled to understand why leaders were chosen for certain roles.

Commonly, in these announcements there was no mention of quantitative outcomes, significant successes published in industry venues and the like that would justify the position match. Simply put, a small group of top leaders made leadership match making decisions based on their perspective of what 'the right fit' was for certain roles.

The purpose of the meeting, previously mentioned, was for top leaders to discuss the organization's decline and strategies for a turnaround. Unfortunately, from that point on the declines in operational outcomes increased. The senior leader at the table determining who was 'the right fit' was a casualty of the environment. His tenure with the organization ended shortly after the meeting.

In the next couple years, the organization started to hire fresh leadership talent. Many new leaders were brought in from the outside while others were promoted from within. The problem was that most (over half) of the leaders did not last long. They started the journey with energy excited about the task ahead. But, their energy and excitement quickly faded when they realized their skill sets were inadequate for the problems.

At one point, the thought leader engaged a senior leader over a large business unit on this topic. This unit was a driver of much of the organization's nonperformance. The senior leader was conducting a national search for a new divisional leader to lead a turnaround. A directive was given by the organization's top leader to fill this role with a leader from the outside even though there were more than qualified internal leaders that could have filled this role.

After months of executive searches, interviews and excessive talent 'headhunter' expenditures, the senior leader announced a new leader had been identified and would be onboarded in coming weeks. Again, this leader stuck to organizational tradition by saying 'Leader 'x' is a good fit for this role.' There was no real explanation or quantitative facts as to why. This left the division and organization as a whole wondering why this leader was the right match for the problem.

The significant part of the equation was the history of the division. In just a few years, the division had multiple leaders in this role that lasted at most two years. The adage of 'revolving door' applies here. Each time one leader left, 'the right fit' was identified and started the journey. Unfortunately, the new division leader was no different. It was like all these leaders were cut from the same mold and senior leaders failed to realize a change was needed.

The thought leader engaged the senior leader by questioning why the same leader archetype was chosen again for this role after it had not worked several times before. The senior leader replied, 'What do you expect me to do, no one else would accept the role.' The thought leader's response was simple, 'You set this leader up for failure, they are not prepared for the role and won't be successful.' Within months after being onboarded, the new divisional leader's enthusiasm began to fade quickly. Operational outcomes continued to decline. This new leader left after only two years and the cycle continued.

The senior leadership again fell prey to insanity. Insanity can be defined as, 'Extreme folly or unreasonableness' (1). It's synonymous with derangement, lunacy or madness (1). In layman's terms, insanity is simply doing the same thing over and over while expecting a different result. If this approach did not work the first few times, why would it work now? In short it did not.

Yet another leader with the same archetype was hired to fill the role again and the journey continued. Shortly after, an organizational restructure occurred. The whole leadership team was disassembled then reconstructed. The takeaway is that one key to top leadership success is being a match maker. There is an art and science to matching the right leader to the right problem. When the match is correct, it's a good fit. When the match is not aligned, it's a high-risk proposition.

THE LEADERSHIP MATCH MAKING WALL

Let's review a simple example of the leadership match making wall as noted in Figure 7.1.

On the left of the image there is a thirty-foot wall. This represents the organization's problem. The higher the wall, the higher the degree of difficulty to fix it. Thus, a greater skill set is needed. As noted, there is only a ten-foot ladder. So, how can a leader with a ten-foot ladder climb a thirty-foot wall?

Let's make it more practical. If the thirty-foot wall represents strategic and system issues of a large division, how will a leader with only tactical or at best operational knowledge solve the problem? In short, they won't. This is the case in the previous dialogue where several leaders cycled in and out of the division over a short period of time.

Simply put, they only had at best operational skills in the face of strategic and systemic problems. They simply were not qualified or prepared for the scope, complexity or challenge of the role. They were essentially set up for failure. So, were these leaders 'the right fit' for the role as announced? Absolutely not.

On the right side of Figure 7.1, there is a thirty-foot ladder and a ten-foot wall. Here, the problem (i.e., wall) is at most operational in nature and less complex than the first example. It simply means the problem is likely tied to a single department or a smaller group of people. Thus, a strategic skill set is not needed as the risk is lower.

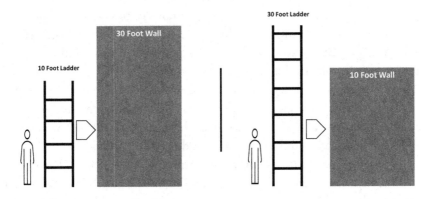

FIGURE 7.1
The leadership match making wall.

The thirty-foot ladder indicates the leader has a strategic skill set. Think of a master change agent. One who has technical skills, operational skills, performance improvement skills, years of experience solving major strategic issues and published outcomes. Why would an organization assign a strategic leader to a much smaller operational problem? The good news is this leader is more than equipped to solve it. But, the leader's full potential is not being utilized. In the Lean world this is referred to as waste (i.e., non-utilized talent). (2)

The takeaway from the exercise in Figure 7.1 is that top leaders must be master leadership match makers. The test is if they can match the right leader to the right problem. If successful, problems will be solved and the organization will perform better. If not, some leaders will be overwhelmed and unsuccessful while others will find themselves bored and underutilized. This will contribute to the leadership revolving door as strategic leaders look elsewhere for a match to strategic problems while operationally minded leaders look for lesser problems to solve. It's a lose–lose proposition if top leaders don't understand what 'the right fit' really means.

LEADERSHIP MATCH MAKING MATRIX

Figure 7.2 is a simple rule of thumb leaders can use to determine 'the right fit.'

There are two attributes: the problem's degree of difficulty and the level of strategic knowledge possessed by the leader in question. The higher the degree of difficulty, the greater strategic knowledge will be needed to address the problem successfully.

As noted in the figure, there are four quadrants or boxes. Box 1 represents a high degree of difficulty and a high level of strategic knowledge needed for resolution. This is a relatively low risk proposition if the right leader is assigned to the role. In short, it's truly 'the right fit.'

Box 2 represents a high degree of difficulty and a low level of strategic knowledge present for a solution. Here, the leader is in a high-risk position. Thus, they are likely to be disrupted in or from their role. The takeaway is that this would be a leadership mismatch and the outcomes would not be desirable.

Box 3 represents a low-risk situation. Here, the problem has a low degree of difficulty. The strategic knowledge needed is also low. The ideal leader for this role would be an operational thinker. Strategic skills would not be required for this role.

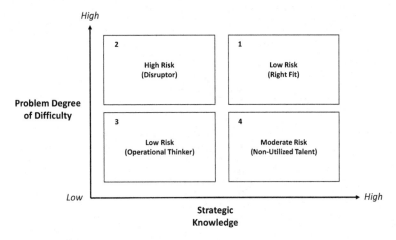

FIGURE 7.2
Leadership match making matrix.

Box 4 is a representation of a moderately risky situation. In this scenario, the problem has a low degree of difficulty while the knowledge available by the leader is highly strategic. This is a mismatch as non-utilized talent will result. The strategic thinker will be underutilized, be bored and likely search for a better opportunity.

The takeaway is that leadership match making is not rocket science, but can be an elusive art. It's imperative that top leaders align the right leadership archetype with the right problem. Anything short of that will be a mismatch and high-risk proposition.

LEADERSHIP MATCH MAKING RISK TOOL

Figure 7.3 is a simple tool leaders and organizations can use to gauge 'the right fit' for leadership match making. Here, a group of leaders is risk scored on several attributes: degree of the problem, strategic knowledge, significant accomplishments, stability of the operating environment and skill set. For high-risk problems that are difficult, leaders would need strategic skill sets proven with large outcomes in difficult environments. This situation would require an integrated skill set comprising technical, operational and performance improvement skills with significant outcomes. As noted in Figure 7.3, only Leader 5 is a right fit and a low-risk proposition.

Leader	Degree of Problem 1-Strategic 2-Operational 3-Tactical	Strategic Knowledge 1-Low 2-Average 3-High	Significant Accomplishments 1-Departmental 2-Enterprise 3-Industry Leading	Operating Environment 1-Unstable 2-Stable	Skill Set 1-Technical 2-Technical+Operations 3-Technical+Operations+Performance Improvement	Risk Score *Sum Columns 2-6 Lower Score = Higher Risk	Risk Level	Match Fit
Leader 1	1	1	1	1	1	5	High Risk	Bad Match
Leader 2	2	2	2	2	2	10	Average Risk	Caution
Leader 3	1	1	2	1	2	7	High Risk	Bad Match
Leader 4	1	1	1	2	2	7	High Risk	Bad Match
Leader 5	3	3	3	2	3	14	Low Risk	Right Fit
Avg Score	1.6	1.6	1.8	1.6	2.0			
Risk Level	High Risk	High Risk	High Risk	High Risk	Low Risk			

FIGURE 7.3

Leadership match making risk tool.

In contrast, lesser degree problems could be handled by operational or tactical minded leaders. The perspective is simple. Bigger skills for bigger problems. As noted in the figure, of the five leaders 60% of them are a bad match. This is largely due to the leaders having high risk problems, marginal skill sets and limited outcomes historically. This group would be categorized as set up for failure due to higher than average risk levels.

Leader 2 is the only average risk match to the role. Across the board, this leader's attributes and their problems are average at best. Thus, the organization would classify them as proceeding with caution. There is enough risk here to be leery, but the risk is limited enough for the leader to be successful with due diligence. It's the equivalent of the probability of a coin toss as to whether the leader succeeds or fails.

SUMMARY

The takeaway is that leadership match making encompasses both art and science. Is 'the right fit' when pairing leaders to problems only qualitative? The short answer is no. Is leadership match making a risky proposition? Simply put, yes. Thus, organizations and top leaders must leverage a measurement tool to ensure they understand, assess, prioritize and mitigate risks associated with addressing their problems.

But, how will leaders be successful in finding the right fit if they don't measure? They simply won't. What leaders and their organizations don't know will harm them, their stakeholders and customers eventually. Ignorance is never bliss.

Although culture is a top priority, leadership match making is also a major component of organizational leadership success. Effective leaders are those that can master the art and science of matching the right leader to the right problem. Anything less is simply a mismatch and a high-risk proposition.

REFERENCES

1. Merriam-Webster, 2022.
2. Institute of Industrial and Systems Engineers (IISE), Lean Green Belt, 2016.

8

Leadership Loopholes:
The Houdini Effect

Harry Houdini is often touted as one of the world's most famous illusionists. He's also known as an escape artist or a stunt performer. In some of his illusion acts he was known for escaping from handcuffs or surviving being submerged in water tanks for prolonged periods of time. In short, he was a master of producing an illusion of the impossible becoming reality.

An illusionist can be defined as 'an entertainer who performs tricks where objects seem to appear and then disappear' (1). Does this concept apply to leadership? Are leaders illusionists? Will leaders have to master the art of escaping unfavorable situations along the career path in order to grow, be promoted and reach optimal success? Is the career journey a straight line up to the top or are loopholes embedded along the way? Is there a formula for success which leaders must follow to successfully escape career loopholes? We will answer these and other considerations in the following.

LEADERSHIP DEFINED

Leadership is a risky business. In layman's terms, leadership is getting others to do what you want without force. Leadership is often synonymous with a title, position, stature, power or control. Do these attributes accurately represent what leadership really means? Arguably not.

There are several leadership archetypes to be encountered along the career path. Some leaders are simply leaders in title only. They may have a title, position or some level of power, but they lack the ability to influence

DOI: 10.4324/9781003439127-8

others, solve problems and achieve results in difficult environments. These leaders tend to be minimally effective. Is someone a leader if they don't have followers? This too is a definite no.

Other leaders are true leaders. Here, the leaders have skill, experience, influence and outcomes. They have the magic ingredients for success and a positive track record of deploying those attributes to help others. These leaders tend to be more effective, stand the test of time and are able to help others reach their full potential if they are willing.

So, what is leadership really? As noted, leadership is getting others to support, follow and champion your vision. It's also using one's talents, gifts and abilities to help others reach their full potential, grow and be successful long term. Leadership is also the ability to get others to do what you want without force. The key is without force. It also involves successfully identifying, solving and preventing problems from recurring.

LEADERSHIP TOLLGATES

The million-dollar question is, how does one achieve the coveted leadership persona? One, leaders learn and grow. In the early years of their career, leaders educate, learn and grow by applying what they have learned. Here, leaders learn by trial and error. The adage of 'the school of hard knocks' applies here. They learn basic skills of how work is done in their organization and industry. They simply master the craft and learn how to work with others to get results.

In mid-career years, leaders continue to learn and start to realize the fruits of their labor. These successes may be operational wins, promotions, stretch assignments, opportunities to present their best practices in industry venues and the like. The key is that years of preparation and growth begin to pay off.

In the latter years of one's career, leaders tend to focus on legacy building. They answer one simple question: What am I leaving behind for future generations? In this career phase, leaders often focus their efforts on the big picture such as impacting the body of knowledge via knowledge sharing. Here leaders often publish their wins and best practices, present at national industry venues or even cross industry events and leave a body of work for the next generation to learn from and build upon.

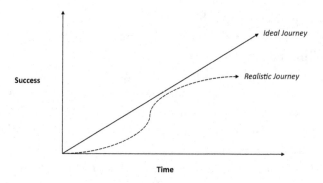

FIGURE 8.1
Leadership career journey.

But, is the career journey a straight shot up to the land of success without any problems? Arguably not. That perception is simply an illusion. (See Figure 8.1 for details.)

Ideally in a perfect world, leaders would succeed all the time from the start of their career to the end. This is represented by the ideal journey line in Figure 8.1. The journey would be a blissful carousel ride in which the leader experiences one success after the other with no opposition, challenges or struggle. Unfortunately, this is simply not reality.

The realistic career journey is also represented in the figure. Realistically, the career journey will have both positives and negatives. There will be seasons of learning and growth as previously described. There will also be seasons of testing where leaders may face challenges bigger than they are. Leaders will also face opposition and competition from peers, superiors and other stakeholders. The journey will include seasons of wins, harvest and promotion for those that stay the course. But, the reality is simple. Leadership is a tough business that has ups and downs along the journey.

LEADERSHIP LOOPHOLES

A leadership loophole is 'a means of escape' (2). When leaders face challenges they will have to find a way around the circumstance to move forward on the career journey or the journey will end. Some loopholes are riskier than others. The test of one's leadership metal is what they do in the face of opposition. Will the leader fold and run away? Will they take what is given to

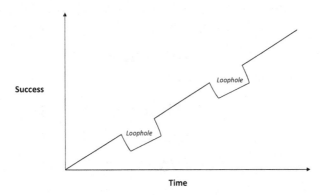

FIGURE 8.2
Leadership loopholes.

them? Will they press through the resistance and overcome? The leadership response to challenges along the career journey will determine the level of success achieved and sustained.

Let's look at Figure 8.2.

Here, the leadership journey realistically has two attributes: time and success. The goal is for leaders to increase in success over time. The longer they maintain leadership roles, the more measurable success they should achieve, produce and share with others. But, this is not always as easy as it sounds.

The career journey, as noted, is fraught with challenges or obstacles. When obstacles appear, leaders will have to remember the Houdini effect and find a way to escape. Thus, the leadership loophole or way of escape appears. During these periods of loopholes, leaders may find their calling to lead others and solve problems at the most challenging time of their lives. Often, leaders will be faced with what appears to be insurmountable odds stacked against them.

But, if successful in navigating the loopholes, leaders will find new levels of success. Challenges and opposition simply represent a test. Tests are often stressful, challenging and difficult. The good news is they don't last indefinitely.

SPONSORSHIP

One of the most common drivers of a leadership test is sponsorship. As leaders move along their career journey they will report to another leader

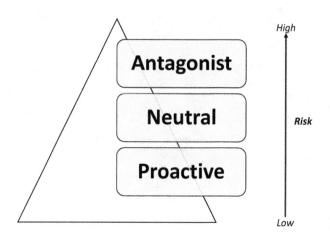

FIGURE 8.3
Sponsor archetypes.

often called a sponsor. The definition of a sponsor can vary. But, a sponsor is simply a leader that guides others along the career journey to a successful end. Sponsors tend to have vast amounts of experience, organizational knowledge, influence and ideally success. Unfortunately, not all sponsors are the same. Some sponsors may be ideal while others quickly become impediments to success. (See Figure 8.3 for details.)

There are a few sponsor archetypes worth noting. Ideally, leaders will have a proactive sponsor. These sponsors tend to have high levels of influence, knowledge and success. Here, these guides help leaders reach their full potential, grow and produce results that pave the way for promotions. These sponsors proactively grow the pie for others and encourage their success. Thus, they are low-risk sponsors and accelerators of leadership growth.

The neutral sponsor archetype as noted in the figure is average risk. Here, sponsors have all the ingredients for success (i.e., outcomes, influence, knowledge, etc.), but do not proactively use them to help direct report leaders. Instead, they are neutral or passive in helping others succeed. If needed or asked, they are likely to help leaders move along the career journey. In reality, leaders that have a neutral sponsor essentially have to figure the path ahead out by themselves.

The third and most unfavorable sponsor archetype is the antagonist. An antagonist is a leader who 'opposes another person' (2). This concept is synonymous with an adversary, opponent, foe or in some instances enemy (2). Will leaders report to antagonist sponsors during their career journey?

Unfortunately, the probability is high that leaders will encounter antagonists along the way.

So, this begs a question. Why would more senior leaders (i.e., sponsors) be an antagonist to their direct reports? There are several drivers here. One, the sponsor may lack confidence in their abilities and view the rising star leader as a threat. Two, the antagonist sponsor may be traditional and favor the status quo. They simply don't like change. The rising star leaders may present a challenge to the way business is done. Thus, the sponsor is adversarial to preserve the current state. Three, there may simply be a personality conflict. Often, people don't mesh. This is an unfortunate but true reality that is often far too common. The key is that antagonist sponsors are high risk and often serve as disruptors to the career journey of others.

LEADERSHIP LOOPHOLE MATRIX

There is a simple rule of thumb leaders can use to test their loophole experiences. See Figure 8.4 for details.

Anytime leaders face a loophole or challenge along the career journey, there are two attributes worth studying. One is the level of sponsorship as noted previously. Is the current sponsor proactive, neutral or antagonistic to the leader's growth and success? The more antagonistic the sponsor, the higher the risk.

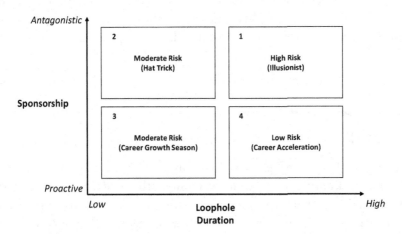

FIGURE 8.4
Leadership loopholes matrix.

The second loophole attribute is duration. Here, leaders can assess risk based on how long the loophole or challenge will last. As noted in box 1 of the figure, when the challenge has a high duration and antagonistic sponsor, the risk is highest. Leaders are at risk of being disrupted in or from their current roles. Thus, they must be illusionists and find a way to escape.

Box 2 represents moderate risk leadership loopholes. Here, the leader has an antagonistic sponsor but the duration of the situation is limited. The course of action should be a hat trick. Think of a magician that pulls a rabbit out of a hat. It's not a full-blown illusion, but simply a solution that gets through the situation. Common tactics could be publishing work to add more credibility, gaining national exposure for the organization and the like. An outside the box loophole is in order to help the leader survive the temporary storm.

Box 3 represents moderate risk to the leader as well. Here, the sponsor is proactive but the duration is limited. Simply put, the leader will have a good sponsor for a short time. The adage of 'make the most of every opportunity' applies here. The leader should view this interaction as a career growth season by answering the following. What can I gain from this sponsor? How can I grow and learn from the sponsor? Are there any short-term wins the sponsor will support during our tenure together?

Box 4 is the ideal loophole and lowest risk proposition for leaders. In this scenario, the best sponsor is involved over the longest time period. Leaders should really leverage their time wisely to accelerate their careers. Here, the goal should be to amass as much exposure, results, relationship growth with other leaders and the like as possible. Access to this level of sponsorship can accelerate career growth and learning and can allow the leader to significantly contribute to the industry body of work which will perpetuate success long term.

SUMMARY

Looking back, leadership is a risky business. Attributes such as skill, knowledge, learning and results determine the leadership career path trajectory. But, one often and equally important driver of leadership success is sponsorship. Sponsors are critical for helping leaders find the right room, gain a seat at the leadership table, find the leadership voice and influence outcomes that will stand the test of time.

At various stages of the career journey, leaders will face challenges that result in loophole experiences. Leaders will have to tread lightly, choose wisely and discern growth opportunities from loopholes that require a Houdini moment of escape. When leaders are paired with ideal sponsors that are proactive, they should leverage those relationships to grow, learn, network with other leaders and amass as many wins as possible. It would be a good time to resume build for future growth and promotions.

When leaders are paired with neutral sponsors that are average risk, they should push through this experience. Leaders must seek out better sponsors even if the relationship is informal. They should also take advantage of any wins they can attain. But, the reality is that nothing lasts forever, that the neutral sponsor will change eventually and that the leader must look for loopholes during this season that will lead to the next season of growth.

When leaders are faced with an antagonist sponsor, they must choose the response wisely. If leaders run away, they will stall their career journey. If they over aggressively resist, they may be disrupted in or from their current role. The key here is for leaders to find ways to continue to add value. At the end of the day, leadership is about using one's talents to grow the pie for others. Even in the face of opposition, if leaders add value, produce results, learn, grow and impact the industry body of knowledge, they become illusionists and escape the danger.

In summary, among the many skills of leadership, being an illusionist should be added to the list. Leaders must master the art of escaping high-risk situations and maximizing low risk at every turn. The career journey is not a bed of roses or a walk through the tulips. In reality, it's a mountain top and valley experience replete with ups, downs, challenges, resistance and opportunities for success. The leadership formula for success is simple: learn, grow, achieve, avoid risk if possible and mitigate risk in a worst-case scenario.

Effective leaders are those that measure, understand risk and proactively elude high-risk situations while capitalizing on low-risk opportunities.

REFERENCES

1. Cambridge Dictionary, 2022.
2. Merriam-Webster, 2022.

9

The Risk of Underestimating Leadership Value

VALUE DEFINED

Value can be defined as anything a customer is willing to pay for (1). *Merriam-Webster* defines value as 'a fair return in goods, services, or money for something exchanged.' From a leadership perspective, what does value really mean? Is leadership value the ability to tell good stories and play politics? Is value in leadership a great resume with industry leading credentials? Does high value for leaders correlate with the ability to implement large scale change successfully? Can a leader be seen as a high value contributor if they save the organization money? We will discuss these and more considerations in the following.

Leadership value is a multidimensional concept. (See Figure 9.1 for details.)

Leaders add value to organizations and stakeholders in various ways. First, they add value through the knowledge they bring to the organization. The knowledge can be cached in innovative thinking, new ways of doing business, published articles they authored, best practices they created and the like.

Irrespective of form there are three levels of leadership knowledge. The first is technical knowledge. Does the leader understand the basic skills required to complete the work? A simple healthcare example may be a pharmacist. Does the director of a hospital pharmacy have a pharmacy degree and understand how to dispense medications?

The second level of leadership knowledge is operational. Here, leaders have some form of understanding and insight related to leading small groups of people, managing budgets, solving problems and dealing with various stressors. The key is for the leader to understand how work gets done (i.e., tactical) and how the business runs (i.e., operational).

DOI: 10.4324/9781003439127-9

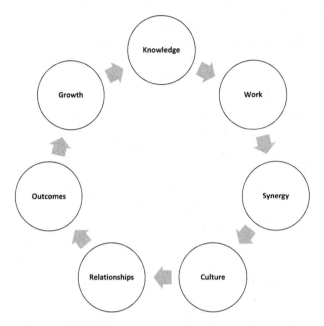

FIGURE 9.1
Leadership value attributes.

The third and ideal level of leadership knowledge is strategic. These leaders are the ideal value contributor in several ways. They tend to understand the work, how to run a business and the overarching strategic challenges facing the enterprise or industry as a whole. Simply put, they can see the forest and the trees. Thus, their value is higher than that of their counterparts.

Leaders also add value to stakeholders through the work they complete. Work can represent making decisions, solving problems, helping others create solutions for their problems and the like. Work can also refer to tactical level tasks that make a business run. In the pharmacy example previously mentioned, tactical level work for the pharmacist would be filling prescriptions whereas operational work could be represented by completing the annual budget.

A third way leaders add value is synergy. Synergy occurs when people accomplish more together than working separately. *Merriam-Webster* defines synergy as 'increased effectiveness that results when two or more people or businesses work together.' The point is simple. Leadership value is added when leaders have a track record of pulling people together, accomplishing work and producing better outcomes from the combined efforts.

Leadership value is also attributed to culture. In layman's terms, culture is simply the way work gets done. Leaders are the overseers of the organization's culture via values and norms. Values are the behavior expectations that leaders place on the organization's stakeholders. These guardrails ensure that the corporate society of stakeholders produce the desired behavior expected to meet and exceed customer requirements. Norms on the other hand represent what actually happens in the work environment. Irrespectively, leaders set culture and culture determines whether or not the organization succeeds or fails long term.

Another attribute of leadership value is relationships. Can the leader establish, cultivate and grow relationships that add value to the organization and its stakeholders? Managing relationships involves establishing trust. Trust encompasses several concepts such as ensuring everyone contributes to success, a focus on producing excellent work and ensuring a safe place for everyone to succeed. Without trust, relationships will fail over time.

The most recognized and often widely regarded measure of leadership value is outcomes. The common expectation here is for leaders to meet operational goals. Does the leader stay within budget as it relates to costs? Can the leader increase revenue streams and exceed these budget thresholds? Can leaders ensure at least 80% of their employee direct reports are satisfied and engaged based on annual engagement surveys. There are many outcome measures that could be discussed. The key for leaders is to set goals, meet goals and improve outcomes beyond base goals.

Finally, leaders add value through growth potential. Here, leaders are assessed on their ability to grow others. Can the leaders produce a crop of next generation leaders via knowledge sharing, training and coaching? Does the leader grow the pie for others by helping them meet their goals, find stretch assignments and get promoted? There are many examples here as well. But, the takeaway is that leaders add value by helping others realize their potential and succeed over time.

FILLING LEADERSHIP ROLES

When organizations and their leaders fill leadership roles, there is a high risk of underestimating leadership value. (See Figure 9.2 for details.)

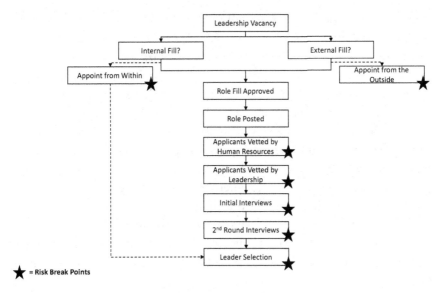

FIGURE 9.2
Leadership vacancy process.

This is a simple example of a process for a large service organization. It's important to note that recruitment processes often are far more detailed. For the sake of conversation and simplicity, the high-level view in the figure will be used.

As noted in Figure 9.2, when there is a leadership vacancy leaders decide to fill the role. Vacancies can occur due to a variety of reasons ranging from retirements to new roles being created. When roles become vacant, there are three decision points. Do we fill the role from the inside, bring in external talent or open the role for both internal and external talent? There is a simple rule of thumb to help with this consideration.

Does qualified internal talent exist currently? If so, promote from within. If internal talent is not readily available, then leaders should look outside the organization. Often, leaders choose to 'fish' for new talent in both ponds (i.e., internal and external talent pools). But, this is risky because if qualified internal talent is passed over for a role they may leave, become disengaged or disillusioned with the enterprise. All of which are undesirable.

There is also another consideration here. Should leaders appoint new leaders for the vacant roles or conduct a vetting and interview process? The answer is complex and organizational dependent. This too is a risky proposition that can go either well or end very badly. Leaders will need to choose wisely here and ensure all qualified applicants get a fair shot at the vacant role if interested.

Once the role is approved to be refilled, the organization typically advertises the role in the appropriate venue to gauge interest from candidates. Some organizations allow their human resources leaders to vet applicants before the final list is given to the hiring leader. Then, leaders are provided with a list of viable candidates for interviews. Some organizations may only have one round of interview while others may choose multiple rounds. This decision depends on the organization's needs.

Finally, leaders complete the interview and vetting processes with a selection decision. The reason for the Figure 9.2 discussion is to outline the risk break points in the process. Each step in the process that is a higher risk is noted with a star. The point is that leaders and their organizations must ensure they understand each leader's value before filling leadership vacancies.

As noted in the figure, there are 11 decision points to fill the leadership role. Sixty-four percent of the decision points or steps are high risk. It simply means hiring leaders are at risk of underestimating candidates' value. There are several risks here worth noting.

If value is underestimated, the result may be non-utilized talent. This is also classified as a waste of resources. Simply put, leaders with great potential may be underutilized. Thus, frustration, turnover or disengagement may follow.

Another risk factor for underestimating leadership value is failure. Some candidates are great talkers, but less than stellar producers. If the wrong leader is placed in the wrong role, then they will eventually fail, have less joy in work and other problems that did not exist are likely to appear. This is essentially a mismatch for leadership.

Inadvertently creating a talent pipeline for competitors is a risk here as well. This simply occurs when leaders do not receive the right role for their skill set and leave the organization. If your organization does not reward talent, your competitors will be happy to do it for you. Thus, leaders must not underestimate or fail to reward high value talent.

A final risk factor for not selecting the right leader is culture. If leaders are not careful, they can easily create an inverse reward system. This occurs when top talent leaders that add value at every turn are not promoted while lesser performers get the roles. Here, leaders and staff lose trust in the organization and its leadership cadre. As trust is lost, excellence in work and operational outcomes decline. The adage of a 'slow operational death' applies here. Thus, leaders must ensure their organization understands value, what it means to leadership, how to reward it and how to measure it.

LEADERSHIP VALUE RISK MATRIX

Figure 9.3 is a simple tool leaders and their organizations can use to measure leadership value.

The matrix has two attributes: outcomes and skill. 'Outcomes' refers to the leader's ability to perform. Do they meet and exceed operational goals? Do they exceed base goals? Can they control costs and maximize revenue? Are they top performers as it relates to quality of service when compared to peers? The key is that leadership outcomes should be measurable compared to industry benchmarks and should be sustained over time. The more the outcomes, the better.

Leadership skill relates to the previous discussion on knowledge. Does the leader have tactical, operational and strategic knowledge or just one attribute? Does the leader have the basic qualifications for the role to understand how the work is done? Skill is a cumulation of technical capabilities, knowledge, experience and education. The more the skill, the better.

As noted in the figure, there are four quadrants or boxes. Box 1 represents a low-risk proposition for leadership value. Here, the leader has a lot of skill and

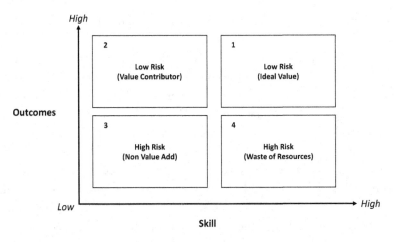

FIGURE 9.3
Leadership value risk matrix.

produces high-level outcomes. Thus, the leader is low risk and the ideal value for a leadership role. These leaders should be promoted, groomed, coached, rewarded, retained and added to the leadership talent pipeline. They should be the first line of promotion candidates to be considered.

Box 2 also represents a low-risk leadership value archetype on a lesser scale. This leader produces high-level outcomes with lower skill levels. Thus, they are a value contributor. These leaders should be upskilled, trained, grown, coached and mentored. They have a lot of potential, but need help realizing it.

Box 3 in the figure represents a high-risk leader as it relates to value. These leaders have low outcomes and limited skills. Thus, they add little to no value. This leadership cadre needs training, upskilling and a management plan. By no means are they ready for a promotion.

Finally, box 4 represents high-risk leaders as well. This cadre is the worst of the bunch. They have a lot of skills with very few outcomes. This is essentially a waste of resources. The organization needs to objectively test these leaders to determine if the issue is a lack of opportunity or the inability for the leaders to perform. These leaders need mentoring, coaching, stretch assignments, a management plan and should be replaced if outcomes don't improve.

LEADERSHIP VALUE RISK TOOL

Leaders may also find value in the leadership value risk tool as noted in Figure 9.4.

The tool simply rates leaders on four attributes. What level of knowledge do they possess? What level of accomplishments have the leaders attained? Do they have more leadership potential that is not being used? Is the leader's skill set being matched properly to organizational problems?

High-risk leaders are those that lack outcomes, knowledge and potential and are not assigned to the right role. In contrast, low-risk leaders as related to value tend to possess more strategic knowledge, have accomplished enterprise wide or industry leading work, have potential to do more and are matched correctly to the organization's needs. The goal is for the organization to promote low-risk leaders as they are the ideal fit and add the most value. In contrast, high-risk leaders add the least value and are not the best choice to fill leadership vacancies.

Leader	Knowledge 1-Tactical 2-Operational 3-Strategic	Significant Accomplishments 1-Departmental 2-Enterprise 3-Industry Leading	Leader Potential 1-Stay at Same Level 2-Do More	Leader Match 1- Skills Not Matched to Org Need 2- Skills Matched to Org Need	Risk Score *Sum Columns 2-5 Lower Score = Higher Risk	Risk Level	Leader Value
Leader 1	1	1	1	1	4	High Risk	Bad Fit
Leader 2	2	2	2	2	8	Low Risk	Ideal Fit
Leader 3	1	2	1	2	6	High Risk	Bad Fit
Leader 4	1	1	2	2	6	High Risk	Bad Fit
Leader 5	3	3	2	1	9	Low Risk	Ideal Fit
Leader 6	2	2	2	1	7	Average Risk	Value Add
Leader 7	3	3	2	2	10	Low Risk	Ideal Fit
Leader 8	3	3	2	2	10	Low Risk	Ideal Fit
Leader 9	3	3	2	1	9	Low Risk	Ideal Fit
Leader 10	3	2	1	1	7	Average Risk	Value Add
Avg Score Risk Level	2.2 Low Risk	2.2 Low Risk	1.7 High Risk	1.5 High Risk			

FIGURE 9.4
Leadership value risk tool.

As noted in the figure, 50% of the leaders are low risk and the ideal fit for vacant roles. Thirty percent are high-risk value propositions and should not be promoted. The remaining 20% add value, but are an average risk for leadership responsibilities. The key point is that leaders don't know what they don't measure. Ignorance is never bliss. Leaders must leverage basic risk tools to understand leadership value before choosing the wrong skillset to solve the organization's problems.

SUMMARY

Looking back, leadership is a risky proposition. Organizations that underestimate leadership value can easily experience buyer's remorse. When evaluating leadership value, organizations should ask four basic questions:

1. What does the leader in question know?
2. What has the leader done?
3. What can they do?
4. How can they contribute to the organization's success?

Simply put, effective leaders are those that can identify leaders with knowledge, measurable outcomes and untapped potential and match them to the organization's needs correctly. Those that can't are at high risk of underestimating leadership value and missing the mark.

REFERENCE

1. Institute of Industrial and Systems Engineers (IISE), Lean Green Belt, 2016.

10

The Risk of Not Focusing on the Right Attributes

THE IMPORTANCE OF TIME

If you were told you had one year to live, what would you spend your time doing as a leader? Would you spend more time in meetings? Would you spend more time glued to a computer or smart device answering e-mails? Would you spend more of your time playing politics vying for the next level role? Would you spend your time in useless conversations and arguments trying to prove your perspective is right? Would you spend more time in meetings (in person or virtual) discussing topics that may not be relevant a year from now?

From a different perspective, if the same scenario was present what would you say your leadership purpose was or is? Would your purpose as a leader be to lead others? Would you say your purpose is to make sure people do their work correctly? Would your purpose of existing as a leader be to manage the organization's resources effectively? All these are noble foci, but are they the best use of a leader's time? Let's see.

One of the facts of life is that time is finite. The career journey is called a journey for a reason. It has a beginning and an end. The stark reality is that in life we have a small window called a career to impact humanity, those around us and the world in which we live. If an average life span is nearly 70 years and an average career is 30 years, a typical leader could spend less than 50% of their life working and leading others. Thus, leaders must make the most of each day.

Would you say you are making the most of your time as a leader? Has or is your time being well spent in leadership roles? If you could get back a few years of your career, what would you do differently as a leader? Also,

DOI: 10.4324/9781003439127-10

what would you do the same looking back? Was it time well spent or a waste of time?

LEADERSHIP FOCI

One of the biggest decisions leaders will make over the course of a career is what to focus on. A focal point is defined as 'the center of activity or attention' (1). There are leadership focal points or foci that add value and some that don't. One perspective is that a value add is anything that a customer is willing to pay for (2). Arguably, value is much more than that.

When determining whether what leaders focus on is a value add, there are several considerations worth noting:

1. Will the customer pay for it?
2. Will the activity benefit others?
3. Can others learn from the focal point?
4. Will the activity increase outcomes and performance?
5. Will the focal point be significant and applicable five to ten years from now?

An answer of yes to all five considerations is time well spent and a true value add. As noted in Figure 10.1, there are several leadership foci that add value.

The first focal point is learning. When leaders spend time learning, it's a good use of time. Learning contributes to leadership growth and allows them to help others.

The second focal point is planning. One of the biggest responsibilities and best use of time for leaders is to plan for the future. Without a vision people and organizations perish. Leaders add value when they plan ahead, create the organization's vision and ensure the right tollgates are on the journey ahead.

FIGURE 10.1
Leadership foci.

A third value add leadership focal point is helping others to improve. Here, leaders grow the pie for others. The goal is to share knowledge, skill and experience to help others meet more goals. Thus, others benefit from the leader's focus on making other leaders and stakeholders better.

Another leadership focus worthwhile is solving problems. There are several types of organizational problems. The most significant problem archetype is enterprise issues. Here, a problem will impact the entire organization and its stakeholders. A good example could be a hospital experiencing difficulty in purchasing enough personal protective equipment for staff to care for thousands of patients due to a supply chain shortage.

Another organizational problem may be divisional. Here, the problem's scope impacts a collection or subgroup of departments. Although important, its impact is limited. A simple example of a divisional problem could be a hospital that is experiencing a nursing shortage. The lack of nursing staff would jeopardize the organization's ability to operate the surgery center. Thus, care and services would be delayed or not accessible.

Finally, departmental issues are the most limited in scope and impact. Thus, they are the least risky. The overarching point is that it's a good use of time for leaders to solve problems.

Lastly, leaders that add value often focus on sharing knowledge. Knowledge sharing is synonymous with knowledge transfer. Here, leaders ensure knowledge is shared from one person to another, across business units, across the enterprise as a whole and even externally. Knowledge sharing may take many forms consisting of, but not limited to, presentations, trainings, published articles, innovative best practices, succession planning, coaching, mentoring and the like. The key is for leaders to share what they know and have improved with others. Thus, the transferred knowledge will allow other leaders to perform better and add value to their customers.

LEADERSHIP FOCUS MATRIX

A simple tool for leaders to determine if foci add value or not is a leadership focus matrix. (See Figure 10.2 for details.)

The matrix has two attributes: Is the customer willing to pay for the leadership activity and will the activity improve outcomes? There are four quadrants in the figure.

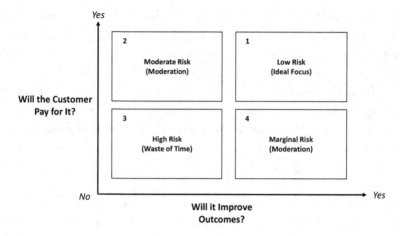

FIGURE 10.2
Leadership focus matrix.

Box 1 consists of a leadership focus that the customer will pay for and improves outcomes. Outcomes can include any operational outcome such as service, cost, quality and the like. Here, the focus is low risk and the ideal time commitment for the leader. Thus, the leader should do more of this and less of other activities.

Box 2 is moderate risk. In this scenario, the customer will pay for the leader's activity focus but it adds little improvement to outcomes. The prescription here is moderation. The leader should spend less time on this activity than those captured in box 1.

Box 3 is a high-risk leadership focal point. Here, the customer is not willing to pay for the focus area and it provides no improvement to outcomes. Thus, it's high risk and simply a waste of time. Therefore, leaders should eliminate and avoid these activities.

Box 4 is also a moderate risk. The customer is not willing to pay for these activities, but the leadership focus improves operational outcomes. The end result is some risk and some reward. The prescription here too is moderation. The leader should spend the majority of time and focus on box 1 and less time on box 4.

So, what's the point of the leadership focus matrix? Time is finite and leaders must choose their time commitments wisely. Some foci add value while others do not. Simply put, time commitments are risky and leaders must minimize risk by finding the best use of their time. The focus matrix is a simple and quick rule of thumb to help with these decisions.

LEADERSHIP FOCUS RISK TOOL

To take it a step further, leaders may find value in the leadership focus risk tool. (See Figure 10.3 for details.)

The tool risk scores for each activity the leaders commit to are based on several attributes: problem solving, helping others, sharing knowledge, learning and planning. As previously noted, leaders spend their time wisely when they are focused on these attributes. The more the time spent on solving, learning, sharing, improving and planning, the more the value is added to stakeholders and more the risk is avoided.

Let's take a practical look at Figure 10.3. In this scenario, there are five activities committed by a leader. Sixty percent of them are high risk and should be eliminated from the leader's calendar. Twenty percent of the focus areas are low risk and the remaining focus area is average risk. The end goal of using the tool is for leaders to assess what they spend their time doing daily, weekly, monthly and annually and select the best use of their time while eliminating high-risk foci.

Leaders should focus most of their time on activities that will solve problems, help others perform better, plan for the future and add value to stakeholders. For low-risk focus areas, leaders should spend most of their time on these activities. Average risk foci would be the next commitment while high-risk time commitments should be avoided.

THE POINT

So, what's the point of the previous dialogue? After over two decades of working with leaders from various parts of the world, it's obvious that many leaders struggle to commit their time wisely. A top leader of a large service industry had been struggling with this concept for years. The leader had been a top operational leader for many years. After decades in operations, the leader was promoted to a CEO position.

The leader was a phenomenal operational leader, but struggled in the new strategic role. For several years, the leader had spent hours daily in the weeds of the business's operating canvas. The weeds consisted of meetings, e-mails, fruitless conversations and the like. As time progressed, the organization experienced an operational downturn. An industry leading consultant was

Activity	Will it solve problems? 1-No 2-Yes	Will it help others improve? 1-No 2-Yes	Will it share knowledge? 1-No 2-Yes	Will it contribute to learning? 1-No 2-Yes	Will it involve planning? 1-No 2-Yes	Risk Score *Sum Columns 2-6 Lower Score = Higher Risk	Risk Level	Leader Value
Activity 1	1	1	1	1	1	5	High Risk	Eliminate
Activity 2	2	2	2	2	2	10	Low Risk	Do More
Activity 3	1	2	1	1	2	7	High Risk	Eliminate
Activity 4	2	1	2	1	2	8	Average Risk	Moderation
Activity 5	2	1	1	1	1	6	High Risk	Eliminate
Avg Score	1.6	1.4	1.4	1.2	1.6			
Risk Level	High Risk	High Risk	High Risk	High Risk	High Risk			

FIGURE 10.3

Leadership focus risk tool.

hired to help the top leader with time management and direction. After a brief assessment, the consultant advised the top leader they were spending too much time on micro issues and not enough time leading.

The recommendation was to spend 80% of the time learning, sharing, planning for the future and executing strategies versus the other activities. The advice was right, but the timing was wrong. The adage of 'a day late and dollar short' applies here. Due to years of not focusing on the right priorities, the leader was displaced and replaced. Within six months, thousands of leaders and staff didn't even remember who the leader was.

This begs the original questions. If a leader was asked if they are using their time wisely, how would they answer? Is their focus on or off target? If they had one year to live or work, what would they spend their time doing? Is the leader's current foci adding value to all stakeholders and will the time commitments be significant five to ten years from now? For the CEO just mentioned, the answer would be no.

SUMMARY

The takeaway from the discussion is that time matters. What leaders do or don't do with their time is critical to their success and the long-term viability of the organization. Once a day is gone we don't get it back. Thus, leaders must ensure time commitments are low risk and add the greatest value to those around them.

But, how will leaders know the risk of focusing on the wrong time commitments if they don't measure? Simply put, they won't. We don't know what we don't measure. Moreover, ignorance is never bliss. What leaders and their organizations don't know will eventually impact them and their customers unfavorably. The adage of 'it's just a matter of time' applies here.

Effective leaders are those that spend time wisely via solving problems, helping others succeed, sharing knowledge, learning and planning for the future. Anything else is a non-value add and simply a waste of time.

REFERENCES

1. Merriam-Webster, 2022.
2. Institute of Industrial and Systems Engineers (IISE), Lean Green Belt, 2016.

11

The Risk of Leading Turnarounds

TURNAROUND DEFINED

A turnaround can be defined as 'a complete change from a bad situation to a good situation, from one way of thinking to an opposite way of thinking' (1). This concept is synonymous with a reversal, improvement, transformation, new direction and the like. Are leadership turnarounds an easy proposition? Can any leader successfully lead an operational turnaround or are special skills required? Can turnaround outcomes serve as both a career ender and a career accelerator? Is a turnaround moment a crucial milestone or rite of passage for change agents? Are leadership turnarounds a risky proposition? We will answer these and other considerations in the following.

In layman's terms, an operational or leadership turnaround typically occurs when outcomes go from bad to worse. These improvement activities can be either proactive or reactive. Think of going to a dentist every six months for a regular teeth cleaning. During a regular exam an x-ray reveals a small cavity that requires a simple filling. This is a proactive example of addressing an issue.

In contrast, a reactive example would be not going to the dentist until a toothache appears. At this point, the tooth is decayed beyond repair and must be extracted. This reactive approach requires a more aggressive and painful resolution that could have been avoided if addressed sooner. As it relates to operational turnarounds, the sooner an intervention is made the better.

There are several types of turnarounds worth noting. The first relates to a simple process redesign. Here, the operation in question may be experiencing low performance tied to operational KPIs (key performance indicators) such as service, cost or quality. The prescription for reversal may be a process redesign that eliminates wasteful steps which add no value to the customer. Think of waiting, errors, reworks and the like. This is the lowest risk proposition for leadership.

DOI: 10.4324/9781003439127-11

A second turnaround example may be both a process and a technology redesign. A simple example could be related to knowledge transfer. A large service organization transitions from using an internally built knowledge management system that houses thousands of policies and procedures to a cloud-based system. The new externally managed system is hosted by a contracted company. This saves thousands of dollars per year in costs and increases customer satisfaction rates of internal stakeholders above 90%. This turnaround archetype poses moderate risk to leaders.

A third and most risky turnaround archetype relates to a total restructure. A good example may be a large service organization with thousands of staff and leaders. For several years, the organization has met progressively fewer goals tied to customer satisfaction, revenue, cost and quality of services. A big change is needed to shift the organization's trajectory or else it faces financial insolvency.

The turnaround prescription here may include a new leadership team, a newly defined governance structure, new technology and process redesign to eliminate millions of dollars of waste. The takeaway is that a restructure has a greater impact and scope than other turnaround archetypes. Thus, its higher risk.

TURNAROUND LEVELS

Leadership turnarounds also have several levels worth noting. These levels are directly correlated to the size, scope and complexity of activities needed to make the current state better. The impact on stakeholders is a factor as well. (See Figure 11.1 for details.)

Figure 11.1 outlines three turnaround levels leaders must consider. The first is a departmental turnaround. Here, the risk to the leader and other stakeholders is the lowest. A simple example could be a small department in a large health system that is experiencing supply chain issues. The supply chain system is riddled with delays, stock outs and other impediments. The department leader chooses to switch the supply chain vendor to ensure staff have supplies needed to meet customer demand. The scope and impact are small. Thus, the risk is low.

The second turnaround level leaders may encounter is divisional. Here, a subgroup of departments is involved. The scope of and impact on the

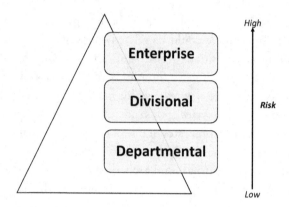

FIGURE 11.1
Leadership turnaround levels.

organization and stakeholders is moderate. Thus, the risk level is higher than departmental.

A simple example could be a large surgery center embedded in a large hospital. The surgery center experiences large staffing vacancies and cannot provide surgical services to meet customer demand. Thus, patients go elsewhere for care. The result is a multimillion-dollar revenue loss for the organization until the staffing crisis is averted.

The highest risk turnaround level is enterprise. An enterprise turnaround requires more resources, impacts more people and is the greatest risk to the enterprise as a whole. Typically, enterprise level turnarounds occur due to years of operational under performance and required very painful prescriptions. Thus, the risk is higher. The adage of 'high stakes poker' applies here.

TURNAROUND RISKS

Along with levels, there are several leadership turnaround risks worth noting. (See Figure 11.2 for details.)

The first risk for turnarounds is failure. It's important to note that each turnaround regardless of level needs a goal or in some cases multiple goals. One risk is that the intervention may not meet the prescribed goal(s). This can be classified as a turnaround failure.

The second risk for leadership turnarounds is retrenchment. Depending upon scope, complexity and impact, there is always a risk that the

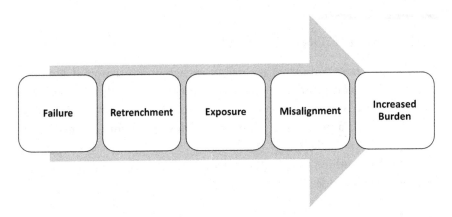

FIGURE 11.2
Leadership turnaround risks.

intervention will make things worse. This is a worst case scenario. Leaders that find themselves in this predicament may easily be disrupted from their role.

The third turnaround risk is exposure. Here, relationship management is key. There is often a risk that hidden weak spots or mismanagement may be exposed due to the turnaround activities. This is a major consideration for responsible leaders needing a turnaround. Leadership jeopardy can easily follow as their competencies are inadvertently exposed. Exposure is often one of the biggest drivers of leadership resistance to change.

The next risk for interventions is misalignment. In this scenario, leaders have the best of intentions to improve a problem. But, the improvements may not be aligned with the organization's vision and future trajectory. A simple example could be to improve wait times at the counter in a fast-food restaurant. If the franchise has future plans to close in door dining and move to online ordering for delivery only, then an intervention would be pointless.

Finally, a significant risk factor for leading turnarounds is the increased burden on stakeholders. A turnaround involves a process. The process ranges from assessments to implementing corrections. The process alone can be very stressful, time consuming and taxing. Also, the solution(s) can impose more work, stress and time requirements if process designers are not careful. The worst thing a turnaround can produce is marginal benefits with more administrative burdens on stakeholders. The adage of 'does the end justify the means' applies here.

THE TURNAROUND PROCESS

Once leaders have considered the risk of engaging in turnaround activities, they must also consider the process. Everything operationally starts and ends with a process. A process is a collection of steps to achieve an end. Merriam-Webster defines a process as, 'a series of actions that produce something or that lead to a particular result' (1).

Figure 11.3 outlines the process leaders should consider when engaging in improvement activities.

The first step is a current state assessment. It's hard to know where to go if one does not know the starting point. The assessment should answer several questions:

1. How is the business unit structured?
2. Is the structure working?
3. Are there structural gaps tied to the organizational chart, functional chart and technology platforms?
4. Is the structure aligned with the organization's vision?
5. What are the main and supporting processes of the business unit?

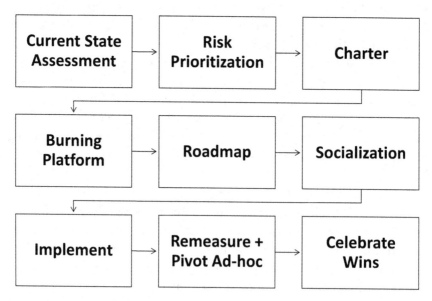

FIGURE 11.3
Leadership turnaround process.

6. Are the processes effective? Simply put, do they achieve the desired end?
7. Are the processes efficient? Simply put, are they customer friendly or riddled with waste such as delays, errors and the like?
8. What is the current state of the people that work in the unit?
9. Are they engaged or disengaged?
10. Is adequate talent readily available to achieve improvement and sustain the wins?
11. Is the work environment stable or unstable?
12. Can the stakeholders meet goals or is goal attainment lacking?

Once the assessment is complete, leaders must risk assess their findings. If something is working and producing the desired end, then it should be categorized as on track which means its low risk. If assessment attributes are not producing desired outcomes and are relatively stable, then they can be segmented as priority. Those items that have significant gaps and are grossly underperforming should be categorized as critical priority. Hence, they have higher risk. Those critical priorities should take precedence and receive attention first.

The next step in the turnaround process is a charter. Here, leaders must outline several key attributes for success. The charter is a formal document outlining the problem, the goal of the intervention, timeline, responsible leadership, barriers and the projected timeline for completion at minimum. It's imperative that each turnaround initiative have proper sponsorship. Otherwise, the efforts will be for naught.

The fourth step in the turnaround process is creating the burning platform. Here, leaders must answer several questions to gain support of stakeholders. The considerations are as follows:

1. What is the change?
2. Why do we need the change?
3. What will it cost?
4. When will it be complete?
5. What resource involvement is needed?
6. What is success?
7. What will be gained by adopting the change?

Once the change has been approved and sponsored, leaders must create a roadmap. The roadmap is essentially the plan that included tollgates for success. The roadmap will include both large and small deliverables for leaders and stakeholders to complete during the turnaround. An effective roadmap will be visually displayed (typically color code for complete, due, past due) and outline what must be completed, who owns it and when it will be completed.

After the plan is complete, leaders sponsoring the proposed turnaround must socialize the forthcoming journey with all stakeholders. Socializing change may range from front-line workers to the governing body. The socialization scope depends upon the size, scope and complexity of the changes. Irrespectively, if stakeholders are not aware of the change to come they may easily resist and the turnaround will fail. The adage of leaders being 'a hero in their own mind' would apply in this scenario.

Once the groundwork is complete, leaders then implement the turnaround plan. Implementation should be well thought out with measurable deliverables on the road map. If noncompliance with the plan surfaces, leaders should leverage the project sponsor (i.e., senior leader) for resolution. Along the implementation journey, it's imperative for leaders to keep a running tally of what worked and what did not work. Later, this information will be greatly beneficial in ensuring success in future turnarounds.

Once implemented, leaders must frequently remeasure predetermined goals to ensure targets are met. Frequency of measurement depends upon the size, scope and complexity of the changes implemented. Some KPIs (key performance indicators) may be measured hourly, daily, weekly or monthly in certain cases. The general rule of thumb is that more frequent measurement is better.

If goal attainment is lacking, it's prudent for leaders to pivot quickly for resolution. Turnaround pivots can range from simple adjustments to a process to redesigning the implementation plan. The greater the pivot needed, the higher the risk for the initiative and its stakeholders.

Finally, leaders must celebrate turnaround successes. Celebration may include, but may not be limited to, presenting results at leadership meetings, publishing best practices or lessons learned, promotions, stretch assignments and monetary compensation as applicable or reasonable. The key is that leaders can never miss an opportunity to reward team success.

LEADERSHIP TURNAROUND MATRIX

When leading turnarounds, leaders can use a simple matrix to assess the risk level to themselves and their stakeholders. (See Figure 11.4.)

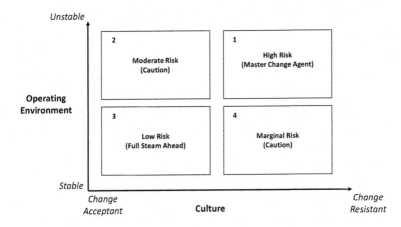

FIGURE 11.4
Leadership turnaround matrix.

The leadership turnaround matrix has two attributes: operating environment and culture. Leaders must answer two questions. Is the operating environment stable or unstable? Is the organization's culture change acceptant or resistant to change?

The more unstable the environment, the riskier the proposition and the greater the chance of failure. Also, if culture is misaligned to change the turnaround will be at a higher risk of not succeeding. There are four quadrants or boxes in the figure as well.

Box 1 is the highest risk proposition. Here, the organization's culture is resistant to change and is unstable. For these turnarounds leaders will need a master change agent. An accomplished and published six sigma black belt is a good example to lead this endeavor.

For box 1 turnarounds, leaders should begin with a charter and strong sponsorship. Also, ensure accountability guardrails and communication channels are present so all stakeholders are apprised of progress or lack thereof. Finally, leaders need to ensure adequate resourcing is readily available to meet the needs of the improvement efforts.

Box 2 represents moderate risk. In this scenario, the organization's culture is aligned to change but the operating environment is unstable. Simply put, the enterprise struggles to meet goals and implement change successfully. Thus, leaders leading the improvement initiative must proceed with caution. Otherwise, risk may disrupt the journey.

Box 3 in the figure represents the lowest risk for a turnaround. Here, the organization readily accepts change and the operating environment is stable.

Thus, leaders should run full steam ahead. This environment has the best chance of success for a turnaround.

Box 4 is also moderately risky. In this scenario, the organization's culture is change resistant which is not ideal. But, the operating environment is stable and less of a risk. Thus, leaders should proceed with caution. If handled correctly, there is a reasonable chance of implementing a successful turnaround. If carelessness arises, the endeavor can easily be disrupted by risk.

LEADERSHIP TURNAROUND RISK TOOL

Leaders may also find a turnaround risk tool helpful as well. (See Figure 11.5 for details.)

As organizations and their leaders consider turnaround activities, they should risk assess each one. As noted in the figure, there are five attributes that are risk scored for each turnaround initiative. These attributes are operating environment, culture, sponsorship, resourcing and organizational alignment.

As previously discussed, higher-risk turnarounds tend to be associated with unstable operating environments and change resistant cultures. Also, neutral or disengaged sponsors and scarce resourcing for turnarounds are higher risk. Organizational alignment, as previously discussed, is also important. Here, leaders must determine the risk as to if the turnaround is aligned with the organization's vision and future direction. If alignment is missing, risk of failure will be higher.

Let's take a practical look at the figure. In this scenario, there are five turnarounds being considered. Sixty percent are high risk, 20% low risk and 20% average or moderate risk. When determining the greatest chance of success, leaders should consider the low-risk propositions first. The low-risk initiatives can be correlated to low hanging fruit. Once the low-hanging fruit is addressed, leaders should then pursue the average risk turnarounds with caution. Finally, the high-risk turnarounds require expert consultation and should be addressed thoughtfully.

SUMMARY

When considering or leading turnarounds, leaders must understand their risk. But, how will they do so, if measurement is not involved? The

Turnaround	Operating Environment 1-Unstable 2-Stable	Culture 1-Change Resistant 2-Change Acceptant	Sponsorship 1-Disengaged 2-Neutral 3-Proactive	Resourcing 1-Scarce 2-Abundant	Organizational Alignment 1-Not Aligned 2-Aligned	Risk Score *Sum Columns 2-6 Lower Score = Higher Risk	Risk Level	Leader Value
Turnaround 1	1	1	1	1	1	5	High Risk	Expert Consultation
Turnaround 2	2	2	2	2	2	10	Low Risk	Full Steam Ahead
Turnaround 3	1	2	1	1	2	7	High Risk	Expert Consultation
Turnaround 4	2	1	2	1	2	8	Average Risk	Caution
Turnaround 5	2	1	1	1	1	6	High Risk	Expert Consultation
Avg Score	1.6	1.4	1.4	1.2	1.6			
Risk Level	High Risk	High Risk	High Risk	High Risk	High Risk			

FIGURE 11.5

Leadership turnaround risk tool.

simplest answer is they won't. Leaders don't know what they don't measure. Ignorance is never bliss. What leaders and their organizations don't know will eventually impact them, their stakeholders and customers unfavorably. Thus, leaders must measure twice and cut once when leading turnarounds and improvement endeavors.

There is a simple rationale worth noting when assessing, prioritizing and selecting turnaround initiatives:

1. Is it the right time?
2. Is the change the right fit for the organization's mission, strategy, vision, culture and operating environment?
3. Can we afford it?
4. Is the expected reward worth the effort? In other words, is the benefit greater than the perceived and actual risk?

Effective leaders are those that find the right prescription for leading turnarounds. Success depends on measuring, understanding, prioritizing and mitigating risk. Risk is a reality directly correlated with change.

As the size, complexity and scope of change increases, so does the associated risk. Thus, leaders that select, cultivate and lead low-risk turnarounds will have the greatest chance of success. Their counterparts will simply become the focal point of the next case study.

The key to successful improvements is to understand the environment, choose targets wisely, craft a good process, implement it flawlessly, measure frequently and celebrate wins.

REFERENCE

1. Merriam-Webster, 2022.

Conclusion

If your career ended by the year's end, what would you leave behind for the next generation of leaders to follow? What would others say you contributed to the industry, to the body of knowledge, to their lives and to the generations to come? Would they even remember you six months from now?

The ultimate test of a leader is:

- How many people will follow you?
- How many will remember you once you have exited the leadership stage?
- How many people did you help during your leadership tenure?
- How much knowledge did you share and leave behind for the next generation?

Leadership is a risky business. In today's world, change is the new normal and only constant. As change grows, so does risk. Thus, leaders must be master change agents and master mitigators of risk. But, how will leaders succeed if they don't measure and lack insight? Simply put, they won't.

Those that are successful in these arenas will ride the waves of success during their tenure on the stage. In contrast, their counterparts will be crushed by the never-ending waves of disruption.

The reality is that time is of the essence for all of us. No one has a forever clock. Leaders must make the most of every opportunity and pay it forward.

In summary, insight and knowledge have power. The only question is, how many leaders will find the keys to unlock the door to sustainable success versus spending their careers running the hamster wheel, wasting time?

Index

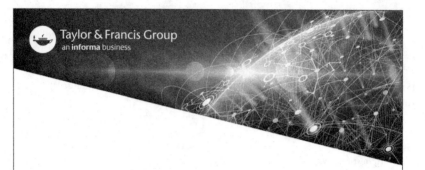

Printed in the United States
by Baker & Taylor Publisher Services